THE PRAYER of Holiness-Hungry People

A Disciple's Guide to the Lord's Prayer

BARRY L. CALLEN

Francis Asbury Press
Distributed by Warner Press
Anderson, Indiana

Coordinator of Publishing & Creative Services
Church of God Ministries, Inc.
PO Box 2420
Anderson, IN 46018-2420
800-848-2464
www.chog.org

To purchase additional copies of this book, to inquire about distribution, and for all other sales-related matters, please contact:

Warner Press, Inc.
PO Box 2499
Anderson, IN 46018-2499
800-741-7721
www.warnerpress.org

Cover and text design by Carolyn Frost.
Edited by Joseph D. Allison and Stephen R. Lewis.

ISBN-13: 978-1-59317-552-8

Library of Congress Cataloging-in-Publication Data

Callen, Barry L.
The prayer of holiness-hungry people : a disciple's guide to the Lord's prayer / by Barry L. Callen.
p. cm.
Includes bibliographical references.
ISBN 978-1-59317-552-8 (pbk.)
1. Lord's prayer--Criticism, interpretation, etc. I. Title.
BV230.C145 2011
226.9'606--dc23 2011024502

Printed in the United States of America.

11 12 13 14 15 16 / EP / 10 9 8 7 6 5 4 3 2 1

Contents

Preface

Christian believers across the centuries have turned to the Lord's Prayer for personal instruction, comfort, and inspiration. It has become the center of public worship and personal living. Some especially mature believers have written their most insightful thoughts about this prayer, and I have sought to drink deeply from the wells of their wisdom. I gladly acknowledge a few of their names and books. References throughout these pages are to their writings. See the bibliography for detail.

Apart from prominent writers, I have studied the Bible again, searching for the deeper truths that nurtured Jesus, a devout Jew, and thus shaped his thinking, praying, and instruction given to his disciples. I also have learned significant spiritual lessons from ordinary believers who had determined to address God and live their lives according to this prayer of Jesus. Some were teachers or pastors, some friends or family members. All were persons of deep faith who happened to cross my path with their graciousness and spiritual wisdom. I am forever in their debt. They are children of the Father who have helped me understand and pray as instructed by the Son and enabled by the Spirit.

The title of this book recognizes that a holy God is calling to a fallen creation, inviting and enabling a restored holiness—the very thing for which our hearts cry out. Jesus taught his disciples to pray in a way that leads toward the Father's high calling and our high spiritual privilege.

I have been a lifelong participant in the Church of God (Anderson), a reform movement inspired by God to re-emphasize the central significance of Christian holiness for all aspects of the lives of believers, and for the life of the church as a whole. During the first decade of the twenty-first century, it also has been my pleasure to participate in what first was called the Wesleyan/Holiness Study Project and then in 2010 formally became the Wesleyan Holiness Consortium. This interdenominational effort has enjoyed the leadership of Kevin Mannoia and in 2006 produced "The Holiness Manifesto" (see Appendix A). Appendix B comes from a 2010 publication of my colleague in the Wesleyan Theological Society, Dr. Thomas E. Phillips.

My friends and specialists in biblical studies, Dr. Barry Ross and Dr. Fredrick Shively, and my wife Jan, a specialist in English literature and grammar, kindly invested valuable time by reading critically the manuscript of this book prior to its publication. While the final text is better because of them, any remaining problems are certainly not their responsibility.

The Lord's Prayer sends us into the very heart of Jesus. It causes us to kneel humbly at his feet, and at those of his and our Father. As we do, we ask to be taught how to pray and live as disciples of Jesus in this troubled world. When we pray properly, and determine to live accordingly through the power of Christ's Spirit, God answers and sets us on the path to holiness. Walking this path faithfully transforms our "here" and graciously destines our "hereafter."

P. T. Forsyth asks a disturbing question in his book *The Soul of Prayer*. "What would happen to the church if the Lord's Prayer became a test for membership as thoroughly as the Creeds have been?" The answer to this question, I fear, would be a great thinning of membership ranks!

Why? Because it would require us to move from a mere mental assent of correct beliefs, *orthodoxy*, to whole-life transformation through God's grace, *holiness*. The biblical promise and our high privilege are that we can both learn of God's truth through divine revelation and participate in the divine nature through life transformation (2 Peter 1:4).

The Lord's Prayer states clearly the expected holiness of God's people—how we should think about God, address God, relate to God, and live transformed lives as enabled by God. So, for holiness-hungry people, this book is a disciple's guide to the Lord's Prayer.

Barry L. Callen
Anderson, Indiana

Introduction

Despite the secularization of recent generations, people continue to pray. Strange as it may seem, secular individuals are showing increased interest in prayer and other spiritual exercises, even though they have proudly "come of age" and never darken the door of any church, synagogue, or mosque. This is despite the fact that any purposeful calling on the name of God is becoming less intelligible and believable to many people.

There is a common perception, even among self-professed Christian people, that prayerlessness is widespread. I suppose this should not be surprising. So many people, including church people, lack a strong sense of God's reality and accessibility. We are extremely distracted by crammed schedules and new electronic marvels. There is little time for any regular attempting of human-divine conversation.

Is there a divine person to whom we can pray? What is prayer? One can speak of it in the most lofty of terms, such as: "To pursue the mystery, to listen and respond to the voice we thought we just heard, to follow the light which beckons round the next corner, to lay hold of the love of God which has somehow already laid hold of us."[1] But our secular culture suggests that we can eliminate almost any mystery by intensifying research on the subject. In other words, there is no need to *pray* if we would just *pay*.

We now have huge electronic ears listening to distant space. So far, we haven't heard any intelligent life out there trying to speak to us. Still, we wonder and listen. Much of the time we are not inclined

1. Wright, *Lord and His Prayer*, 11.

to lay hold of the love of God because we have no clear sense that it already has laid hold of us. Why speak to one who seems not to be responding, perhaps because he has no voice or just isn't there?

Prayer is a very confused subject in our times, even among traditionally religious people. We are not praying, and yet we have new interest in praying; we have less sense of a God to whom we might pray if the need arose, but we long nonetheless for human wholeness (holiness). In all of this, the biblical witness remains clear—and its word is countercultural to say the least. Here is the ancient witness: God is very real, and conversing with the divine is possible and central to Christian faith and life. God has spoken. We are invited to hear and respond. Jesus has taught us the proper attitudes of prayer and the content of prayers that truly please God.

The Bible resorts to the language of metaphor for describing God. What else could mere humans grasp? It speaks of God as "Father" and highlights the dialogic dimension of God's nature, desires, and actions. God speaks, listens, invites human response, interacts, initiates, and responds. A covenant between God and humans has been established by divine initiative, especially in the coming of Jesus Christ. We now have the opportunity of being bound in a sacred relationship, a partnership where both parties have roles and voices and ears.

I heard an interview with Billy Graham some years ago in which the interviewer, looking for a good story line, asked, "Sir, do you believe in the old-time religion?" Graham paused, obviously pondering the trick question. Finally, he said, "Yes, I do, if it's old enough!" His response was wise.

Before he answered that interviewer, I imagine Dr. Graham thought of his beloved North Carolina, the religion of his own parents, grandparents, and neighbors he knew. He may also have been mindful of the numerous radio and television preachers filling the modern airways. He wisely saw the limitation of understanding his faith within the particulars of place and people and then applying that to others in all times and places. He knew that religion and location strongly shape each other. So his thought raced to the biblical base of the Christian faith. If one intends to go that far back, then Graham was all for the "old-time" religion.

What happens in these pages is similar to Graham's response. Where we go for understandings of God, holiness, and prayer is back to the original fountain of truth, the Lord Jesus himself. Jesus did not give his disciples all the particular behaviors of faithful discipleship; he did, however, give the theological foundations, enduring principles, and action guidelines that are essential and timeless for Christian life. He did so in part by sharing with his first disciples a model prayer for those of us holiness-hungry people who need sure guidance for the praying of our prayers and the living of our days. Since God has given us a voice and is willing to hear our prayers, we need to listen carefully to Jesus so that we will know how and for what to pray.

We need to be sure we are reaching back to the religion of the Bible when a subject like Christian holiness is involved. We must come to terms with holiness because it speaks of God's essential nature, God's desire for our human experience, and thus the context in which true prayer functions best.

Holiness is of central importance to all Christians in all times and circumstances. Holiness tends to be conceived woodenly in terms of behavioral dos and don'ts that seem appropriate in a given day and place, but then become quaint and almost humorous to people of later times and other places. In these pages, we will consider the meanings of Christian holiness as they arise in relation to the Lord's Prayer. And arise they will!

As I wrote in a 2008 book, "Holiness, according to the Bible, is defined by the very nature of God as that is understood best in Jesus Christ. Further, the scope of holiness is not restricted to spiritual elites, believers who are especially emotional, or those who hope to escape this world by being radically different and safely disconnected. To the contrary, according to the Bible, holiness is for all who believe in the biblical God made known through Jesus Christ and who are willing to be part of what God intends, the redemption of this present world."[2] I concluded with this: "People today are hungry for a

2. Callen, "Context: Past and Present," 9.

faith community with a difference, a people who really care, love, and serve, a congregation that is clearly different because it knows and walks with a holy God."[3]

Jesus sought to satisfy that holiness cry in the hearts of his disciples of all generations. Otherwise, they would not be mature and effective agents of his holy Father in this world. Therefore, he taught them—and now he teaches us—how to pray about who we must be and what we must do. The prayer instruction of Jesus points to the very heart of what it means to be a Christian. For serious believers in Jesus Christ, understanding, using, and actually living the prayer he taught his disciples is not optional. It is the God-inspired pathway of faith and life. It is the pathway that Jesus pioneered and now has given to us. He was ablaze with God's purifying fire, and he tells us to wait until sparks of that holy fire rest on each of us (Acts 2:1–4).

Finally, a word of explanation. I use the phrase "the Lord's Prayer" throughout this book to refer to the content of Jesus' prayer instruction to his first disciples, found in Matthew 6 and Luke 11. The phrase is common. I readily admit, however, that in some ways it would be more accurate to call it "the disciples' prayer." Jesus designed it for the use of his followers, not himself. It includes a request for forgiveness of debts / sins, something hardly needed by the sinless Jesus. Even so, the spirit of the prayer is characteristic of Jesus' own intense prayer life—and all of it is to define our own.

Many Christians refer to this prayer as the "Our Father." The Anglican communion, for instance, calls for of its communicants to use the "Our Father" in their daily prayers and standardized forms of worship at holy communion, confirmation, marriage, and burial of the dead.

Probably no words from the mouth of Jesus have been more studied, revered, and repeated by Christians over the centuries than those of the "Our Father" or the "Lord's Prayer." Jesus had just warned his disciples not to pray by heaping up "empty phrases as the Gentiles do" (Matt 6:7). Jesus then gave them a disarmingly brief and humble prayer—no arrogance or futility of vain repetition here. Rather than *empty phrases*, Jesus gave his disciples prayer phrases

3. Ibid., 17.

that were *very full indeed*. This is why we now give them such serious attention.

The Request

The disciples had a request for Jesus:
"Lord, teach us to pray." (Luke 11:1)

CHAPTER 1

Lord, Teach Us to Pray

Prayer is a universal religious phenomenon. Even so, Christians of every generation have felt the need for guidance in the practice of prayer. It was so with the very first disciples of Jesus: "Lord, teach us to pray" (Luke 11:1). It was the gracious response of Jesus that we call the "Lord's Prayer." That provision for all the prayer needs of those first disciples is for us as well.

Of course, the first question, basic to all else, is this: Why pray at all? The writer of Hebrews explains that "without faith it is impossible to please God, for whoever would approach him must believe that he exists and that he rewards those who seek him" (Heb 11:6). So prayer holds the promise of great spiritual reward. To receive it, however, we must believe that God is, hears, loves, and stands ready to respond to all who approach in the manner suggested by Jesus.

Let's admit it. Most Christians have difficulty with prayer. In fact, we rarely engage in it except for some perfunctory efforts at "blessing" meals or trying to listen to and agree with a pastoral prayer on Sunday morning. Occasionally, the Lord's Prayer is announced as part of a worship service. Respectful worshipers loyally follow along, mostly from memory, hardly thoughtfully, and usually concerned about whether this time they are supposed to say "debts," "trespasses," or "sins."

Busy people tend to leave things like prayer to the clergy. Some ministers, not that mature themselves in the practice of prayer, secretly wish that the task could be left to nuns, monks, and seminary professors. Some say that they are not "mystics" given to nonrational "piety." However, professors have their own problem: An academic preoccupation can insulate them from *experiences* of the faith. As for monastics, either behind or outside church walls, Thomas Merton, Henri Nouwen, and others have found that not all prayer problems go away just because their lives are dedicated to prayer.

Even if we have sincere faith and a desire to learn to pray, problems persist for many of us. Paul says in Romans 8:18–27 that we don't know how to pray as we ought. We don't know what to pray for, so we need to depend on God's Spirit to help us with prayer. It is not easy to attempt dialogue between the God of the universe and lowly people caught up in the mundane problems of this crazy world of ours.

Some Christians assume that God doesn't need our prayers, since all that will happen has been determined in advance by the unalterable divine will. They believe our prayers cannot change things. If God is truly sovereign, what could prayer possibly change? "What will be will be," with or without our prayers.

R. C. Sproul leans heavily in this direction. He believes in God's full sovereignty and complete control, insisting that "no prayer of any human being ever uttered in history ever changed the mind of God in the slightest, because His mind doesn't ever need to be changed."[1] So why pray? Sproul stands with John Calvin in this respect, believing that prayer is not so much to influence God as to influence the one praying. Prayer is invited by God. If it has any effect on the outcome of a situation, it does in a very limited sense.

Many of us, however, read biblical revelation differently. We find the Calvin-Sproul view much too restrictive, drawing a wrong implication from the fact of divine sovereignty. It reflects improperly on God's being and working in the world. Sometimes, according to the Bible, we *have not* because we *ask not* (James 4:2). Scripture describes a wonderful "concurrence" when God and we work together, mysteriously interacting for the fullest effectiveness. I see in the Bible a less meticulous divine predestination, less evidence that God exercises advance control of all particulars, than Calvin and Sproul see. I see

1. Sproul, *Prayer of the Lord*, 14.

more openness on God's part to the prayers of his people, more readiness to respond, more willingness to work cooperatively with his praying children.

Living in a House of Prayer

If this more "open" view of God's activity in the world is accurate, prayer is critical indeed to our Christian lives. It means that many redemptive things will remain undone because—and only because—we fail to intercede with God. Prayer *can* change things. Even if we accept the more limiting view of prayer espoused by Calvin and Sproul, we have to admit that prayerlessness deprives those who pray.

Here is the most important reason for a life of prayer, particularly when the Lord's Prayer lies at its center. An active life of prayer is essential to the process of being *with* Christ: in order to become *like* Christ, with the result of learning to live *in* Christ's special way. A central goal of any Christian believer is spiritual formation, moving toward maturity in Christ. The teaching contained in the Lord's Prayer sends us in the right directions and nourishes our deeper life of holiness.

For centuries, devout Christians have found in the Lord's Prayer the fundamental elements to direct their search, the needed building blocks of spiritual formation. Let it be said directly: The people of God have no higher calling than to realize their commission to be a *house of prayer* (1 Kings 8:22–53; Isa 56:7). The key to the front door of this house lies in this prayer of Andrew Murray:

> Lord Jesus! Reveal me to the Father. Let His name, His infinite Father-love, the love with which He loved Thee, according to Your prayer, be in me. Then shall I say aright, "My Father!" Then shall I apprehend Your teaching, and the first spontaneous breathing of my heart will be: "My Father, Your Name, Your Kingdom, Your Will!" Amen.[2]

2. Murray, *With Christ in the School of Prayer*, 23.

The goal is that we be faithful in the school of prayer with Jesus, our teacher. In this way, the holy God will share the ways of holiness with us.

However, much too often we are elsewhere—even we who believe. Our congregations tend to be places focusing on fellowship and fun, religious performances and moral platitudes, altruistic fundraising and good works. In the middle of all this activity, none bad in itself, prayer is relegated to formalized speeches in worship services, pious products of the paid clergy, and lines projected on giant screens for people to repeat aloud as prompted. Many churches are less houses of prayer and more places of religious routine and tradition. This is not what Jesus had in mind! He was very concerned about the waywardness of his people, so he called them to a life of faithful obedience.

Jesus was a loyal Jew well aware of the traditional prayer practices of his people. First-century Jews prayed daily in carefully prescribed ways, including use of the *Shema* (Heb., "hear"), which begins with the words, "Hear, O Israel: The Lord is our God, the Lord alone" (Deut 6:4–9). Then there were the *Shemoneh 'esreh*, eighteen prayers or benedictions, the content of which ring throughout the Lord's Prayer. The first benediction begins with, "Blessed art thou, O Lord our God." The third says, "Thou art holy, and thy name is holy, and holy beings praise thee daily." Prayer six entreats, "Forgive us, O our Father, for we have sinned." The ninth prayer says, "Bless this year unto us, O Lord our God, together with every kind of the produce thereof, for our welfare."

Then there was the *Kaddish* (Aramaic, "holy"), a prayer used regularly in synagogue worship and sometimes compared to the Lord's Prayer. Jesus likely would have known it by heart. It reads: "Magnified and sanctified be His [God's] great name in the world which He hath created according to His will. May He establish His Kingdom during your life and during your days, and during the life of all the House of Israel, even speedily and at a near time, and say ye, Amen!" One translation says, "May He give reign to His kingship in your lifetimes."

Taken together with the Psalms, a prayer book of the Jews, Jesus and his fellow worshipers had a rich and wonderfully conceived system of regular prayer. Jesus did not condemn the system, but the common use of it. The best instrument of spiritual discipline can slip so easily into formality, duty, glib recitation, and thoughtless use. The Jews had their ancient warning in Ecclesiastes 5:2: "Never be rash with your mouth, nor let your heart be quick to utter a word before God, for God is in heaven and you upon earth." Jesus likewise warned his disciples (Matt 6:5).

Being rash, hasty, or just negligent about prayer is a weakness of all religious communities, not just the Jews. We are told in Acts 19:34 that pagan worshipers in Ephesus stood for two hours crying out in mindless repetition, "Great is Artemis of the Ephesians!" The prayer wheels of Tibet spin with their tiny paper prayers fluttering in the wind as Buddhist worshipers seek to get answers for their much filling of the air. Some Muslims are known for repeating sacred syllables, on occasion for hours on end. The Jews sometimes did that with *Shema*, almost replacing prayer with a religious self-hypnotism. One way not to pray, therefore, is to act as though the practice is some kind of churchly magic. We cannot manipulate God with proper phrases and pious postures.

There also is the problem of praying with wrong motives. Some of the Pharisees of Jesus' day had developed the habit of praying at length in public to build a reputation of great piety. They were praying, not so much to God, but to passersby who would see and appreciate their efforts. Again, let's be careful about pointing fingers. It happens in all times and places. A Christian preacher is reported to have prayed an elaborate and seemingly endless morning prayer before his congregation in Boston. One person later said that it was possibly the most eloquent prayer ever offered to a Boston audience! How God may have received this prayer is unknown.

Jesus wanted his disciples to avoid any further burdening of the Father's tired ears! Their praying was not to be fancy, endless, calculated, or crowd-pleasing. They could not earn divine attention by the emotion, verbosity, or logic of the prayers themselves. Instead, the disciples' prayers were to be childlike—not childish, but humble—the kind of prayers that would stick in the throat of the proud. If their prayers were to reflect Jesus and be taken seriously by the Father, they had to be couched in reverence, admit to ignorance (even helplessness), and ask only for the glory of God, necessary bread, and needed forgiveness and redemption. All the while, they should demonstrate a readiness to forgive others, a willingness to live by God's standards, and an eagerness to pursue their destiny as loyal members of God's kingdom.

The Plurality of Prayer

Do you hear the plurality in the "they"? The disciples of Jesus asked how they were to pray. The model prayer given by Jesus in response does not begin with, "My Father." It begins with "Our Father." This plurality signifies two things, complementary and both very important.

The first is that a Christian does not approach the Father alone, as an isolated human trying to contact the eternal. Jesus himself authenticates the prayer that God will hear because our approach to the divine throne of the Father is accompanied by the active presence of the Son. Jesus told his disciples, "I will do whatever you ask in my name, so that the Father may be glorified in the Son" (John 14:13).

By the way, note that the Lord's Prayer does not end with "in Jesus' name." That qualification is included from the very beginning of the Lord's Prayer. That phrase, "*our* Father," frames the entire prayer. As Paul put it, "for through him [Christ] ... both of us have access in one Spirit to the Father" (Eph 2:18). Jesus tells us to go into our private room and shut the door before we pray (Matt 6:6), in order to avoid the arrogance and hypocrisy of the Pharisees. He does not advise us to cut off our spiritual life from the faith community.

The second significance of the opening plurality of the Lord's prayer involves the church. Christian prayer before the Father, as well as our life in the Son by the Spirit, is not to be characterized by isolation, aloneness, or independent thinking and acting. The deeper walk with the Father must be taken in company with God's people. To abandon the body of believers is to undermine ourselves; to deny the great cloud of witnesses, the saints of the ages, is to be spiritually impoverished. Jesus calls for the community's participation in prayer. He teaches a shared spiritual quest in which God works through each disciple to bless the others.

There is always an awareness of the church, the company of believers, in Jesus' prayers. He demonstrates that we must not engage in lives of prayer that deny "the most fundamental reality of our humanity; that we are made in the image of God—the Lover, the Friend, the Relational One."[3]

In the Western world of the early twenty-first century, individualism is rampant. Results trump relationships. We see failed communities on every hand, including divided churches where an awkward togetherness has spawned much pain, division, and failed mission. People long for the shared intimacy of true community, but they also fear being manipulated and injured by self-serving structures. "Mainstream" churches have been declining in part because they are thought to be too much in the business of maintaining themselves and too little in the business of giving themselves away for the sake of Jesus.

Jesus' use of "our" language is most inviting, but also cautionary. The intent of Jesus seems clear. To truly be *in him* and pray properly to his Father, our prayers must be characterized by *community*. We cannot love God and be out of touch with our brothers and sisters (1 John 4:20). We cannot seek personal holiness and disregard the practical unity of Christ's body (Eph 4:3–6). In fact, holiness is the key to true unity. We cannot enter meaningfully into the life of the Triune God without engaging seriously in the life of the Christian community (Phil 2:1–2).

Sisters and brothers in Christ need the spiritual gifts resident in each other. Our broken and bleeding world needs to see the Christ community that looks beyond the human barriers of gender, social class, skin color, and nationality, leveling the field before the cross of Jesus. Christians are to be known by how wonderfully they love each other, even their enemies! They are to know and act like "there is no longer Jew or Greek, there is no longer slave or free, male and female, for all of you are one in Christ Jesus" (Gal 3:28).

3. Timms, *Living the Lord's Prayer*, 34.

To see the world through the eyes of Jesus, we must begin to pray with the reconciling grace of "*our*." How natural this was for Jesus, the Jew, who knew from childhood that one's identity before God was bound up in being a member of the called people of God. How clear Jesus was. The people of God includes more than traditional Jews. In fact, some of them are not included just because they are Jews.

As Jesus is indescribably intimate in relation to the Father, so he prays that we believers might be an intimate faith community. This is to be God's worldwide community, an "unnatural" and amazing fellowship of love. The church comprises all believers together in Christ because of the unifying grace of God. Jesus prayed, "As you, Father, are in me and I am in you, may they also be in us" (John 17:21).

Entering the Private World of Jesus

Matthew 4 describes how Jesus had been isolated in the desert for an extended time and suffered a set of severe temptations from the devil. This text is particularly significant because only Jesus could have reported the experience. His disciples later learned about his temptations because he had decided to tell them. In his judgment, their knowing about his private experience would be critical to their own faith lives.

N. T. Wright observes something similar about the Lord's Prayer: "When Jesus gave his disciples this prayer, he was giving them part of his own breath, his own life, his own prayer. The prayer is actually a distillation of his own sense of vocation, his own understanding of his Father's purposes."[4] That sense of vocation was surely sharpened for Jesus in the wilderness of temptation. This Prayer is a lens through which we can see, in a condensed fashion, how Jesus was reading and responding to his times, how he was grasping his own unique identity, how he was looking to his Father for perspective, direction, and courage to proceed on a dangerous mission—and how *not to proceed*.

---

4. Wright, *Lord and His Prayer*, 2.

The Prayer ushers us inside the very private world of Jesus so that we can glimpse the holy heart of the Son yielding to his Father—and wanting so much for his disciples to do the same. This Prayer brings us to holy ground! It becomes holy for us when we actively pray Jesus' Prayer ourselves, first with our mouths and then with our lives.

Remember that the Lord's Prayer was given in response to an urgent request of Jesus' disciples. They were trying so hard to get things right, to find the way ahead, especially if something should happen to Jesus—as he kept hinting that it would. How would they ever manage? What would they need to know if suddenly he were gone from them? So they posed their big question: "Would you teach us how to pray?" The answer of Jesus has become classic for Christians of all times.

This Prayer contains the right elements, motivations, theological bases, requests, and attitudes for every Christian disciple. It is brief and easily remembered, and yet it contains all things fundamental to proper life in God. It is a treasure beyond measure, an essential guide to the life God intends. The intent of Jesus is not to teach about prayer in the abstract; it is "to correct false notions regarding communion with God, and to advance the disciples in a knowledge of the Father as revealed by the Son."[5]

The Prayer that Jesus offers is brief and childlike. One would think that a prayer intended to plot the path to communion with God would be a substantive and theologically intense essay. In fact, it has only seventy-two words in Matthew's original version of the Greek, and even fewer in Luke's version. But the simplicity and brevity of this Prayer can be very misleading. This is *not* a child's prayer. Below and between every word, it is theologically rich and life demanding indeed.

The two New Testament settings where the Lord's Prayer appears (Matthew 6 and Luke 11) both make abundantly clear that it is a *disciple's* prayer. It is "not just the spiritual version of the baby's mug and spoon set, though it is surely that as well. It is the suit of

5. Zodhiates, *Lord's Prayer*, 37.

clothes designed for us to wear in our full maturity."[6] This Prayer is intended for those who are already following Jesus, who have some basic spiritual understandings and commitments, but who are both longing for more and are at a loss to know how to proceed from where they are. It is, in fact, a *holiness* prayer.

Communion with the holy God spawns a deepening desire for that divine holiness to spill over into one's own life. The grace of *justification*, bringing from God forgiveness of past sin, only whets the spiritual appetite for the grace of *sanctification*, maturing in God's love and assuming the very likeness of Christ. God calls for this—"you shall be holy, for I am holy" (Lev 11:45). Paul saw this need and prayed for God's provision: "May the God of peace himself sanctify you entirely; and may your spirit and soul and body be kept sound and blameless at the coming of our Lord Jesus Christ" (1 Thess 5:23).

The questions are many. How should one order priorities, find that spot where the waterfalls of God will spill over one's head like a cleansing fountain, learn to stand and pray in a way that encourages being "sanctified entirely"? How should we even ask, pray? Where, how, for what? Learning to be a Christian involves learning to pray as a Christian. We might say that a mature Christian is one who has learned how to pray the Lord's Prayer thoughtfully, yieldingly, and trustingly. We also might say that Christian holiness comes when one prays this prayer of Jesus with his or her *whole life*. No wonder, then, that out of the mouths of would-be disciples come the words, "Lord, teach us to pray!"

Those first disciples had watched Jesus' own prayer life, how he would minister wonderfully to crowds and then withdraw to pray. They had become aware of the relationship of his intimacy with God to his effectiveness with the people, of his prayer and then his power. They wanted this secret to invade them also. What exactly did Jesus pray when he was off by himself? What did he expect in their prayers? How could they survive when persecuted, and how could they manage to minister like Jesus?

Asking Jesus how to pray is a prayer in itself: "Lord, lead us immature disciples on your holiness path that moves us toward the

6. Wright, *Lord and His Prayer*, 12.

fullness of life." If sin is "the orientation of the whole person away from God, then holiness is the whole person turned in love to God… Holiness is personal fellowship with a personal God…Holiness is the love relationship of a person with the holy God…Holiness is following our living Lord by his grace and help."[7] Holiness is deliberate openness to the Spirit of God so that the Spirit can help us become more like Jesus day by day.

Surely our praying should not be primarily for satisfying our all-too-human desires for long life, riches, and fame. It should be for submission to the will of God and transformation by the grace of God—our holiness, in other words, which in turn will satisfy God's highest will for us. The first three petitions of the Lord's Prayer, in fact, involve placing God first. That is the necessary first step toward holiness.

Jesus teaches us to bring the whole of our lives humbly before God so that he can begin to pour the richness of his own life into the whole of us. God loved us first and chose to come to us while we were yet sinners. Jesus himself is doing the prayer instruction, so we can truthfully say that "we don't choose this prayer; it chooses us. It reaches out to us, forms us, invites us into the adventure called discipleship…We know the truth by coming to know the person, and we know this person [Jesus] by learning to pray as he taught us."[8]

7. Kenneth E. Jones, *Commitment to Holiness*, 73, 6, 167, 4.

8. Willimon and Hauerwas, *Lord, Teach Us*, 16.

Discussion Guide

1. Is the active and meaningful practice of prayer a problem in your church? Is it a problem in your personal walk with God?
2. According to Jesus, how should his disciples *not pray*?
3. If God is truly sovereign, does prayer really matter? Can it change anything if God has predestined all things?
4. Why are the wilderness temptations of Jesus so important to us?
5. How might Christian "holiness" be defined? Are you satisfied with the definition given in this chapter? How can the Lord's Prayer help you reach that high spiritual goal?

Two Versions of the Lord's Prayer

Matthew 6:9–13	Luke 11:2–4
Our Father in heaven,	Father,
Hallowed be your name.	Hallowed be your name.
Your kingdom come.	Your kingdom come.
Your will be done,	
On earth as it is in heaven.	
Give us this day our daily bread.	Give us each day our daily bread.
And forgive us our debts,	And forgive us our sins,
As we also have forgiven our debtors.	For we ourselves forgive everyone indebted to us.
And do not bring us to the time of trial,	And do not bring us to the time of trial.
but rescue us from the evil one.	

CHAPTER 2
Pray, Then, Like This

Did Jesus intend that his disciples of all times should constantly recite the Lord's Prayer, repeat its exact words by rote? Certainly not. Even so, this particular prayer is our spiritual foundation. It is the Christian pattern for proper living as well as proper praying. The message of Jesus is that our prayers will be acceptable to God only when they fit this pattern—when they reflect its attitudes, thoughts, and desires. Although we are not told to recite it verbatim, every prayer of ours should express the Lord's Prayer in one form or another.

While the apostle Paul told us to pray without ceasing (Eph 6:18; 1 Thess 5:17), Jesus tells us to pray without deviation, faithful adherents to the lofty vision of Jesus' own prayer. "Here are the ideas that undergirded his ministry as the Messiah. Here are the hopes which kept him moving against the tides of opposition. Here is the purpose of his life that took him to the cross at the last. We meet Jesus himself more in the Lord's Prayer than at any point in his teaching."[1] So we listen closely when Jesus says, "Pray, then, like this."

Upon analyzing the Lord's Prayer, one quickly realizes how intentional and comprehensive it is. Just as there are seven distinct colors in the spectrum, there are seven distinct movements in praying the Jesus way:

1. Laymon, *Lord's Prayer in Its Biblical Setting*, 53.

1. *Approaching* God in adoration and trust;
2. *Acknowledging* God's work and worth in praise and worship;
3. *Admitting* sin and seeking pardon;
4. *Asking* that basic needs be met, for ourselves and others;
5. *Arguing* with God for blessing;
6. *Accepting* from God one's own situation as he has shaped it; and
7. *Adhering* to God in faithfulness through thick and thin.[2]

Another way of seeing this prayer's comprehensiveness involves the seven petitions in the prayer. The first three, the so-called "Thy" petitions, are worship requests that seek to focus reverently on God: (1) may the divine name be hallowed, (2) may the divine reign come, and (3) may the divine will be done. Initially, we are to ask, not for our sake, but for God's.

The fact that the first three petitions deal with God indicates that "this should be our first concern when we pray. We should center our prayers upon God Himself, for God is the center of the universe and of all things, not we. This is the basic lesson we learn from the Lord's Prayer."[3] Only after proper focus on God do we proceed to ask for four very human needs: bread, forgiveness, avoidance of temptation, and deliverance from evil.

There is yet a third way of appreciating the Prayer's comprehensiveness. Christianity stands on three sturdy legs that have withstood the tests of the centuries. One summarizes the Christian way of believing (Apostles' Creed); the second summarizes the Christian way of behaving (the Ten Commandments, seen through Jesus' Sermon on the Mount); the third summarizes the Christian way of communing with God (the Lord's Prayer). Of the three, the Lord's Prayer compresses so much into the fewest words. It provides the most succinct answers to the basic questions that God puts to us

2. Packer, *Praying the Lord's Prayer*, 17.

3. Zodhiates, *Lord's Prayer*, 42.

as we journey through the joys and sorrows, pains and pleasures, doubts and questions of our faith lives.

The Lord's Prayer shapes the ideal conversation we disciples should be having with God. This conversation proceeds as follows:

Divine question: Who do you believe that I am?
Disciple's answer: Our Father in heaven.

Divine question: What do you want from me most of all?

Disciple's answer: The hallowing of your name, the coming of your reign, to see your will be known and actually done.

Divine question: To pursue those worthy ends, what do you ask for now?

Disciple's answer: Bread for strength, pardon for sin, protection from temptation.

Divine question: How can you be confident in my ability and willingness to provide such things for you?

Disciple's answer: Because yours is the kingdom, and the power, and the glory, forever and forever!

The final question and answer admittedly do not reflect words found in the earliest texts of the Lord's Prayer, but they are fully justified for use here. (See more on this in chapter eight.) In these divine questions and human answers we perceive the heart of the ideal divine-human conversation. The Lord's Prayer both asks the big questions of life and gives the best answers. It portrays proper communion between Creator and creature, between Father and children.

Praying as Jesus directs is the equivalent of Jesus' taking a loaf of bread and saying to his disciples, "Take, eat; this is my body" (Matt 26:26). He says, in effect, "My dear disciples, you should receive and digest this particular prayer into the very bloodstream of your spiritual lives. It is central to my heart and vocation, and it is the foundation of the proper perspectives, attitudes, and petitions of my wise and faithful disciples!" To use words attributed to Martin Luther: "The Lord's prayer is the highest, noblest, and best prayer; all other prayers shall be suspected which do not have or contain the content and meaning of this prayer."

Limitations of Human Language

The Lord's Prayer lies at the heart of the Sermon on the Mount, a composite of the teachings of Jesus. The version of the Prayer found in Matthew is preceded by two warnings from Jesus. First, don't use your prayers to show others how religious you think you are (Matt 6:5–6). Second, don't just "babble" meaningless words (Matt 6:7–8). Proper prayer is not designed for public show and personal pride.

One major word featured in the Prayer taught by Jesus is *Father*. For it not to be meaningless for us, or to convey the wrong meaning to others who might hear, careful definition of the word is necessary. While the importance of this word in the prayer of Jesus is explored in chapter three, something needs to be said here as a disclaimer. Critics in recent years have decried the Prayer's use of the word *Father* as prejudicially male language that does not convey anything positive to the many women who have endured terrible human fathers. They have a point, of course, and we are told that as many as thirty-four percent of American young people go to sleep in a home where there is no father at all. Enduring a terrible father or experiencing the absence of a father is hardly how Jesus wants disciples to think of and experience God!

Let it be noted, however, that we human beings must use anthropomorphism when addressing ultimate things. That is, we draw from our own human experience, from what we know, and then use that experience and its associated language in reference to that which is beyond our experience, what we do not know in the usual ways and for which we have no satisfactory language. Therefore, "until we redefine our natural assumptions of what a father is and is not, we cannot receive the revelation that Christ offers us in his prayer to *our heavenly Father*. Unless we deprogram our concept of father, the Holy Spirit cannot reprogram it."[4]

With this frank admission of how humanly biased and inadequate our language is, we acknowledge openly the volatile history of our God language. For example, ancient Judaism was a patriarchal culture not nearly as sensitive as we now are to gender equality. That culture's God-language is reflected in the biblical writings. To some degree, and as people always do, biblical writers had to frame the mysterious *out there* in terms of the known *down here*. For instance, there is no clear Hebrew equivalent for the English word *family*—probably the closest is *bet ab* ("father's house"). However, God is not a man or a woman. The profound reality of God outruns our ability to capture it on paper. Even so, we proceed as directed by Jesus. It's the best we have. We pray not to a cloud or star, not to a principle or thing, but to "our Father."

This language gap is acknowledged in the prayer of Jesus with the phrase "which art in heaven." The God so wonderfully near us in Jesus remains always more than we can conceive and verbalize. God is the One separated from, different from, all else. God is above the crowd, beyond the ordinary, outside our language limits. Even so, Jesus conveys in his prayer instruction that this dramatic separation is now bridged!

The divine Father does indeed abide in heaven and thus differs greatly from us, without being hopelessly remote from us or inaccessible to us. Using language of geographic location (God is "up there") is inadequate in the face of our advanced astronomy. Rather, God exists "in heaven" in the sense that God is and functions, not in a different *place*, but on a different *plane*. In fact, holy as God is, the Great Beyond is also *right where we are*, loving us as a perfect father would.

So, prayer—communication and communion with God as revealed in and by Jesus—is natural, possible, wonderful! When it clashes with our experience of failed human fathers, the advice of R.C. Sproul is helpful: Focus on the word before *Father*, on the *our*.[5]

4. Hart, *"R" Father*, 25.

5. Sproul, *Prayer of the Lord*, 26.

The great Father who is related to all of us humans is not the individual father we may have known who violated fatherhood through neglect or abuse. Our Father in heaven is the fatherhood standard, the judge of faltering earthly fathers, the One ready and able to bring to us the love, comfort, and security we may never have known from the man who sired but did not and would not love us.

Here is the very heart of the Christian faith. The perfect Father, the One transcending all our earthly experience, has become visible to us and accessible to us in Jesus. And what we learn about the Father from the Son is that we love others only because God has first loved us! This is amazing and truly transforming.

Praying to a Holy God

Jesus, our prayer teacher, begins our instruction by telling us to focus on the *holy God*. We will not pray properly unless we begin with a deep reverence for the Holy One to whom we are daring to speak. Before the kingdom of God can come on earth the way it now is in heaven, and certainly before the divine will can be done on earth the way it already is in heaven—indeed, before we can be transformed into persons different from this world, different as God's character already is and always has been—the name of God must be *hallowed* in our hearts and by our words. This hallowing is exactly where Jesus begins his teaching on prayer.

The proper prayer begins with humility in the face of the Holy. The fundamental assumption of proper prayer is that of the divine holiness; the fundamental prayer goal should be a realization of this holiness right here on the earth, beginning with the transformation of each of us who dare to pray to "our Father who is in heaven."

The Lord's Prayer, our faithful spiritual guide as Christian disciples, is an unmistakably *theocentric* (God-centered) one. Daniel Migliore has it right: "By calling us to attend first to God's honor and reign, and by summoning us to see ourselves—our needs and our desires—in relation to God's purposes for the whole creation, the Lord's prayer continually reforms our spirituality and our theology."[6]

6. Migliore, *Lord's Prayer*, 2.

Since that's the case, he concludes, "Just as Christians would lose their identity if they no longer attended to the proclamation of the gospel, the celebration of the sacraments, and the ministry of compassion to the needy, so the practice of calling upon God is for Christians as necessary as breathing in and out."[7]

Central and necessary as prayer might be, however, it is hard to practice for sinners who, while freshly impacted by divine grace, nonetheless remain immature spiritual beings caught in the web of secular surroundings. Even the great apostle Paul struggled, saying, "We do not know how to pray as we ought" (Rom 8:26). Yet he announces that, despite our ignorance and surroundings, we do not pray *alone*. "The Spirit helps us in our weakness…intercedes with sighs too deep for words" (Rom 8:26–27). The great prayer of Jesus "can only be prayed by the Holy Spirit already within us and already having made us heirs of God and joint heirs with and in Christ."[8]

Jesus promised that his Spirit would come "and will guide you into all truth…He will glorify me, because he will take what is mine and declare it to you" (John 16:13–14). Jesus had assured his disciples of this: "When they bring you before the synagogues, the rulers, and the authorities, do not worry about how you are to defend yourselves or what you are to say; for the Holy Spirit will teach you at that very hour what you ought to say" (Luke 12:11–12). The path to Christian holiness involves learning to pray by being filled with the Spirit, who is prepared to pray in, through, with, and for us. To pray properly is to pray "in the name of Jesus"—that is, to pray in line with his nature and spirit, in unison with his vocation, in loving concert with his other committed children.

Praying to a Triune God

Although a fully articulated theology of the divine Trinity was a few generations away from those first disciples, Jesus offered them a Trinity prayer.[9] According to Jesus, we are to pray: (1) to the One

7. Ibid., 1.

8. Crossan, *Greatest Prayer*, 26.

9. I once organized a systematic theology the same way (*God as Loving Grace*, 1996) by demonstrating that the Trinity is the God who *Stands* (Father), *Stoops* (Son), and *Stays* (Spirit).

standing sovereignly above us as holy Father, whose name we are anxious to hallow; (2) to the One who once stooped below to be savingly with us in Jesus as the Holy Son, and whose life we are anxious to share; and (3) to the One who always remains with us to teach, comfort, guide, and empower as the Holy Spirit, whose presence is our wisdom, power, and hope.

Romans 5:5 catches all of this Triune theology: "God's love [Father] has been poured into our hearts [Son] through the Holy Spirit that has been given to us." Martin Luther catches it all in another way, saying that the ancients defined prayer as an *ascensus mentis ad Deum*, a "climbing up of the heart unto God." This Trinitarian theological breadth is found in the elements of the Lord's Prayer. Everything essential to the life of faith is there: right relationship with God, right worship, right citizenship, right partnership, right stewardship, right fellowship, and right discipleship.

We are to pray like that! And when we do, we must be diligent in avoiding ever-present distractions, even religious ones. Anyone who has traveled in the homeland of Jesus has seen the virtual adoration of places, the near worship of sacred sites—inaccurately located as some of them may be. Tourists say, "If only I could walk where Jesus walked!" But that hope can lead to either an enrichment or corruption of faith.

Perhaps this is why the Lord's Prayer in Luke 11:2–4 is prefaced by an ambiguous note on time and place. The Gospel writer says Jesus taught his disciples the prayer "in a certain place." Maybe the exact location was not identified lest we hallow it! Maybe the Holy Spirit "didn't want us to know the exact place [or] we would have sanctified the ground on which our Lord prayed and where He sat to teach His prayer."[10] We are not to build shrines on holy spots so much as celebrate the presence of God everywhere. We are to focus on the content of the Lord's Prayer rather than become lost in the words, metaphors, or locations of the Prayer. If we are to get lost, let it be in the wonder of God the Father, the glory of God the Son, and the constant presence, guidance, and power of God the Spirit.

10. Zodhiates, *Lord's Prayer*, 29.

Discussion Guide

1. How can we best deal with the problem many people have with the word *Father* in the Prayer taught by Jesus?
2. Explain at least two ways in which the Lord's Prayer can be seen as comprehensive, including the whole Christian faith and life.
3. Review the ideal conversation between God and a Christian disciple—the divine questions and the human answers listed in this chapter. Is this how you talk with God? If not, why not?
4. The Trinity is a classic doctrine of the Christian faith. How might it shed light on our prayer life?
5. Have you been to a "holy" site? Are sacred sites an aid or distraction to true faith? Where was Jesus when he taught his disciples how to pray? Does it make any difference?

Hebrew word for Yahweh, the great

"I am who I am."

CHAPTER 3
Our Father in Heaven

In the twenty-first century, the "I's" have it. Whether iPhone, iPad, MySpace, or a thousand TV commercials insisting on *my* rights and *my* needs being met, the omnipresent cultural standard is "I." In our intense self-orientation, many of us now have a problem with our very belief in God. We do not genuinely pray without believing in the One to whom prayer is directed. Our great advances in science have not always led to great advances in moral goodness or spiritual maturity. Too often, we have used advances in science to build more sophisticated weapon systems to use against each other.

This sad fact suggests that our civilization is characterized by cynicism, no purpose for prayer, and no place for God. The mixed message of a church bulletin conveyed the problem humorously: "The morning sermon will be 'Jesus Walks on Water.' Tonight's sermon will be 'Searching for Jesus.'" There it is. We affirm our belief in the divine and then wonder if our belief is actually baseless. Jesus is amazing! But can we find Jesus? Do we even need God for living in these days of ours?

When we make no place for God because we assume no need for such a place, there comes a chilling reality to those hard words of Thomas Hardy: "The dreaming, dark, dumb Thing / That turns the handle of this idle show."[1] Is that an accurate description of life in our world? Is that all there is? Does the empty vacuum of our times encourage us to live as though *I am* and *God is not*? When the

1. Thomas Hardy, *The Dynasts*, Spirit Ironic in the After Scene.

vacuum of self-centeredness becomes intolerable, Jesus reminds us that he is the bread of life, the water we can drink and thirst no more, the presence of God actually among us and for us, the reason why prayer is possible and meaningful.

God makes prayer possible by coming to us and revealing himself as a Person seeking loving relationships. The beginning of the Lord's Prayer has three elements that answer correctly three key questions about such a relationship. They are the "Father," the "our," and the "in heaven." The first indicates *to whom* we should pray, the second those *with whom* we should pray, and the third *why* we should pray.

Vision of the Transcendent God

The biblical perspective on prayer is rooted in its understanding of God: "The vitality of prayer lies largely in the vision of God that prompts it."[2] With God, all things are possible! But when we lack this vision of the divine, prayer is impossible.

The Lord's Prayer is sometimes compared to the Ten Commandments, because each seeks to clarify the essential nature of faithful life within the context of a proper understanding of God. Those ancient commandments were not isolated rules for living. They were grateful responses to God's actions among his people. "I am the Lord your God, who brought you out of the land of Egypt, out of the house of slavery" (Ex 20:2). *Therefore*, God was saying, "respond in the following ways (the "commandments") and you will be what I saved you to be, my people reflecting my character and my will in all of your lives. Do it out of gratitude and joy, not out of blind and grudging obedience."

Isaiah "saw the Lord" in the year that King Uzziah died (Isa 6). That's when a vision of the divine usually comes. The destruction of some idol, some death, some experience of extremity, some shaking of life's traditional foundation will turn our eyes toward God. The 9/11 terrorist attack in New York City, for instance, was followed by a large upswing in church attendance, albeit short-lived. Our current

2. Packer, *Praying the Lord's Prayer*, 35.

Western culture is less than favorable for divine sightings. It tends to worship "at the altars of consumerism. Its temples are shopping malls. Its priests and priestesses are Madison Avenue executives. Its sermons are television commercials. Its saints are people with six-figure incomes [or more!]. Its annual pilgrimage is the Christmas shopping season. Its logos are designer labels."[3]

In such a consumerist culture, we communicate constantly, but say little of lasting significance. Prayer waits on the death of another king, a fallen idol, or the arrival of some disaster that finally strikes deep enough that we finally look up. When we do look up, we scan the skies for anything that is not just another idol vulnerable to crashing. We long to see the unseeable, conceive the unconceivable, speak of the unspeakable, name the only One beyond names. How difficult and rare that is! But that's precisely where Jesus begins his prayer teaching.

When God told Moses to lead the people out of Egypt into freedom and divine destiny, Moses insisted on knowing God's name. His people and the pharaoh would want to know what god had dared to launch such an audacious redemption. What Moses was told left him in a paradoxical and almost speechless awe: "I am who I am" (Ex 3:14). God, the Father in heaven, is beyond all categories that can be named. He is what he is, does what he does, and needs answer to no one. That ineffable God is the One who had decided to save the people of Israel!

Let's put this divine paradox into theological words. God is *holy*, which literally means "other," beyond all we can know in normal ways. Therefore, God is wholly *sovereign*. Moses learned this when God answered his question. Yet there is more. The Sovereign One has become our *Savior*. Jesus said to his disciples that he was the fleshly expression of the loving heart of the Father, God himself now present to save! This vision of God naturally leads us to prayer.

Christian theology would develop over the centuries a doctrine of Trinity as a way to confess, in multiplicity and yet in complex singularity, the amazing God now known in Jesus Christ. This doctrine captures an awareness of the God whom Jesus says will lead one to

3. Seamands, *Holiness of Heart and Life*, 37.

proper prayer. Leo Gafney summarizes wisely that which is as real as it is awesome:

> In praising the name of God, we recall that we have been allowed to contemplate a most mysterious secret—that in the inner life of God there is love, relationship, and community. God is father and mother and creator of all. God is also redeemer coming to our rescue when most needed. God is sanctifier bringing love and courage. How this can be we do not know. We know only that we experience God's varied effects in our lives, and we share the love that comes from within the Trinity. In wonder and awe we bless God's holy name.[4]

Spiritual Intimacy with the "Father" God

Because the Lord's Prayer introduces the "Father in heaven" who is also "our Father," it is a family prayer. Christ came "not just to redeem us but to restore us to proper relationship with God and with one another...He's giving us an introduction to our greater family—the true body of Christ—and an initiation into a new way of living."[5] Mature prayer involves renouncing self-centeredness and reaching out both to God and to our new brothers and sisters in the faith. To celebrate the incarnation, God being fully with us in Jesus, we must allow our fellow believers, our fellow worshipers and prayer partners, to walk with us in our brokenness, even as we actively walk with them. It is "through this lens of family, this relationship with God and with one another, that we move deeper into the Lord's prayer and, more specifically, into our Father's heart."[6]

Jesus belonged to a rich praying tradition. He could assume that his disciples cared about prayer, knew well Isaiah's dramatic vision of God (Isa 6), and hoped to share in something like it themselves. They still weren't sure where Jesus fit into the whole of their Jewish tradition, but they were open to learning. Jesus had a teachable moment

---

4. Gafney, *Guide to the "Our Father" Today*, 33–34.
5. Hart, *"R" Father*, 17, 18.
6. Ibid., 21.

to work with—and he surely didn't waste it! He began with his dramatic awareness of God.

Traditional Judaism made occasional references to God as "Father" (e.g., Isa 63:16). Jesus was a Jewish teacher who came to fulfill and not destroy his rich religious heritage. He deliberately continued and expanded the "Father" tradition, using this manner of addressing God no less than six times in his classic high priestly prayer recorded in John 17. He knew himself to be God's "Son," a unique relationship indeed. Therefore, "Father" was an appropriate God reference, at least for him. His identity gathered into itself both the salvation and mission of Israel. Salvation (freedom) had come to Israel, God's first-born son (Ex 4:22–23). Slaves were released from their bondage to sin and transformed into children of the divine.

When Jesus called God "Father," historic memories and meanings were shaken awake in his Jewish disciples. They watched and listened to Jesus, their teacher, and were beginning to understand him to be their Lord.

"We think we get it!" Get what? "He [Jesus] wants us to get ready for the new Exodus. We are going to be free at last! This is the Advent hope, the hope of the coming of the Kingdom of God. The tyrant's grip is going to be broken, and we shall be free."[7] The Lord's Prayer was a culmination of many generations of Jewish hope and the launching of a new day of actual fulfillment. Jesus' disciples were to become nothing less than the liberated messianic people! The kingdom of God was to come *in them* and then *through them*, all in the name of this amazing Jesus.

In a very real sense, we are to pray out of our own sense of amazement about who God is, as revealed through Jesus. John Killinger says: "For Jesus to call God our heavenly Father was to make the most audacious theological statement that could ever be made. Think about it—the God who created the world and cast the nebulae in space; the God who heard the prayers of the first man and woman on earth and who sees the intricacies of the future; the God whose majesty is seen from the highest mountain and who inhabits the jeweled depths of the darkest ocean; the God who led

7. Wright, *Lord and His Prayer*, 15.

the Hebrews out of captivity in Egypt and spoke when Jesus was baptized, saying, 'This is my beloved Son, listen to him'—*our Father.*"[8]

Using the name "Father" to address God may have been appropriate for Jesus, but why would he direct his disciples to do the same? If Jesus really was the expected Messiah, what was he implying about them? Was Jesus assuming that his disciples—including us today—are somehow *participating* in sonship with the divine and in the mission of Israel? The amazing and wonderful answer is "Yes!" Consider this scene. A disciple of Jesus walks right into the presence of God and, with shyness but also with an outrageous boldness, says, "Hi, Dad. Please, may I, too, be considered an apprentice son?"[9] Ridiculously arrogant? No, because the disciples could add this: "Jesus, your Son, sent me and told me I should ask you this."

Jesus was taking a great risk. His own people considered his claim to having a special relationship with God an awful blasphemy, and finally they would have him crucified by the Romans for it. The foreign power then in military and political control of God's people cared little about charges of religious blasphemy, but Rome reacted quickly if it smelled a simmering revolution. To be intimate with God means to march to a different drummer. In some cases, it also means paying the consequences imposed by authority figures who will not tolerate someone's being out of step.

Speaking of Jesus, John the Apostle concludes that "to all who received him, who believed in his name, he gave the power to become children of God" (John 1:12). Paul puts it this way: "God sent his Son...so that we might receive adoption as children" (Gal 4:4–5). Having God as our "Father," then, involves our being God's children as the result of being adopted into the Son. That's why we disciples are to pray in the name of Jesus. It's only in him that we have access to the Father as his children, by faith and adoption. And being in him means being part of God's family, the family we call the "church."

The Lord's Prayer, then, is for Christians only. It is for believers who are loved by the Father as the Son is loved, sinners now adopted

8. Killinger, *God Named Hallowed*, 19–20.

9. Wright, *Lord and His Prayer*, 20.

into God's family by divine grace. This adoption brings a double realization: that we are deeply loved and that nothing in all creation will ever be able to separate us from the love of God in Christ Jesus our Lord (Rom 8:39). Such realizations should send us to our knees in gratitude and joy.

And there is even more. Because we are adopted children of God through Christ, the Son, we are granted the gift of the Spirit of Christ in our reborn hearts. The Spirit joins Jesus in prompting us to cry out in trust and expectation, "Abba! Father!" (Gal 4:6). This paternal term demonstrates deep intimacy with the divine. "Something less familiar feels more appropriate...but the gospel calls us to a family reunion, not a meeting with the CEO."[10]

Jesus was well aware that this word *Father* gathered up all the meanings of Israel's vocation as the special people of God. Moses had confronted Egypt's pharaoh with this: "Thus says the Lord; 'Israel is my firstborn...Let my son go that he may worship me'" (Ex 4:22–23). Once freed, the slaves of pharaoh became the liberated children of God. They were to serve as God's good-news people, a shining light to the nations, the freed race spreading freedom and the rejoicing people spreading the joy of God to others. They were liberated children of the Father—and now Jesus was suggesting that his disciples embrace their own liberation from sin, and prepare themselves for the final exodus. This time it was to be fulfillment of the Advent hope, the coming of Messiah, the realization of the reign of God among the chosen and in the whole of creation.

Reigning God

So Jesus begins sharing the ideal prayer for the citizens of the coming kingdom. The very first words of this Lord's Prayer, whether in Greek or Aramaic, are "Our Father." They convey all of this salvation history, all of this expectation, moving beyond intimacy with God to revolution through God. The reign of God is about to begin over all the fragile little kingdoms of humans. God had promised King David that from his family line would come a child to rule over God's

10. Timms, *Living the Lord's Prayer*, 56.

people, and the reign of that child would have no limits or ending. God would be this child's "father" (2 Sam 7:14). Jesus was saying to his disciples, "I am that child! In me, you also are children of God. I am Messiah and, through me, you are messianic people. You are in the family line that roots in God and one day will reign over all that is or ever will be!"

The Jews of Jesus' time knew that the oppressions they had suffered under Assyria, Babylon, Persia, Greece, Egypt, Syria, and Rome would eventually come to an end. Prophecy foretold that Messiah would come, finally liberating God's people. The questions were How? and When? The answers of Jesus were, "Through me," and "Now!"

This is why Jesus begins this model prayer for his disciples by addressing "our Father." All things begin with the sovereign One, the liberating and saving One, the Messiah-sending One. If the word *Father* catches up all this history, frustration, expectation, and adoption, Jesus was saying to his disciples, "Let it be *now*, and let it be *us*!" Begin your prayer, he said, with "Our Father." The Father of Jesus is also our Father, not only the Father of Israel and of Jesus, but ours too! He is Lord of Lords, King of Kings, the author of time, the bringer of salvation, and the master of eternity.

God's reign is indeed coming on this old earth, and we disciples are to pray that the dramatic change begins here and now with us. Our awareness of this revolutionary mission as the messianic people of Jesus is the beginning of our awareness of being holy, both as individual believers and together as the people of God. Praying as Jesus does not simply make us comfortable in our faith since the Father is on our side; it throws down a revolutionary gauntlet, demanding that we be on God's side, no matter what happens to us.

For us, the kingdom now is a family matter. We are no longer our own. Through this Jesus, we now belong to the Father and are to be changed into the likeness of the Father, becoming a small taste of the total reign of God that one day will be all in all. We have received the message of the Messiah. "It is the Exodus-message, the message that tyrants rightly fear. Most revolutions breed new tyrannies; not this one. This is the Father's revolution. It comes through the suffering and death of the Son."[11] It is a kingdom like no human kingdoms. It is actually a divine family.

This prayer of Jesus is a family announcement. For all who receive God through Jesus, God grants "the power to become children of God" (John 1:12). Jesus may be the Son of God in a unique way, but Paul told the philosophers in Athens that "in him we live and move and have our being" (Acts 17:28b). Jesus, the only-begotten (Gk., *monogenes*) Son of the Father, the sole one with the full right to address God as "Abba, Father" (Mark 14:36), grants his disciples in his Prayer the privilege of using such a personal, familial address in approaching God. When we become children of God, it becomes both proper and possible for us to call God "Father."

Addressing the True God

Since we are adopted through the Son, we are called to share with the Son the pain of the world so that the world might be healed. Praying with our Lord, and being mindful of our Father's nature and mission, we are in effect asking that we be made apprentices of the Son, initiating with him the coming reign of God the Father. We are signing on as agents of the Son through the empowerment of his Spirit. We pray, "Dear God, make it so, whatever the costs, whatever the risks."

This is the true path of Christian spirituality, the highway to holiness, growing into the Father by daring to impersonate the Son. Jesus said to his followers, "As the Father has sent me, so I send you!" (John 20:21). When we pray the Prayer beginning with "our Father," we are inviting and celebrating God's full reign here and now, and asking that it might first appear in us.

We disciples of Jesus seek access to the divine throne and ask for God's attention because Christ promises that we will be received warmly and lovingly, as a father receives his beloved children. The twin truth is that "fatherly love, on the one hand, and transcendent greatness on the other are two qualities in God that the rest of the [Lord's] prayer assumes at every point."[12] The Lord's Prayer "starts

11. Wright, *Lord and His Prayer*, 19.

12. Packer, *Praying the Lord's Prayer*, 21–22.

by addressing God intimately and lovingly, as 'Father,' and by bowing before his greatness and majesty. If you can hold those two together, you're already on the way to understanding what Christianity is all about."[13] The Holy One, the Father, has begun to share qualities of the divine nature with undeserving but nonetheless beloved children.

Jesus insists that "we must always remember that the God to whom we pray is a God of love who is more ready to answer than we are to pray...We do not come to a God who has to be coaxed, or pestered, or battered into answering our prayers. We come to one whose one wish is to give."[14] However, when we look carefully at the Jewish liturgical references to God as "Father," we find much more than a simple affirmation of the available intimacy and generous intent of the Creator for the creature. Divine fatherhood implies far more than comfort for our lonely and hurting selves.

In this respect, we may say that the Lord's Prayer is a both/and prayer. There's a world yet to save, a price yet to pay, a mission yet to fulfill. But there also is a holy God whom we must hold in awe and wonderment, even while we rejoice in God's nearness, tenderness, and grace-filled accessibility. Disciples of Jesus are to move back and forth between the sheer otherness of the great God, whose being is in the eternities and whom we must therefore hold in reverence, and the amazing intimacy of this God's presence in Jesus Christ and his Holy Spirit. "His presence without our awe produces a sappy familiarity on our part. Our awe without His presence results in a meaningless and lonely spiritual quest. Neither leaves us satisfied or fulfilled."[15]

By addressing God as "our Father" who is "in heaven," we place emphasis on twin realities that too often are separated in church life. There is the intimate reality of our dear and loving Father who is so present with us in healing, gifting, and empowerment. There also is the sovereign reality of the God who is utterly different from us, whose ways are higher than our ways. Jesus makes clear that our prayer life must balance both these realities. God is in heaven, yes,

13. Wright, *Lord and His Prayer*, 7.

14. Barclay, *Lord's Prayer*, 12.

15. Timms,. *Living the Lord's Prayer*, 69.

but also very close at hand. He is in heaven, yes, but nonetheless a very present help in time of trouble. He is in heaven, yes, but we can feel his immediate and wonderful presence in our most trying circumstances.

Because this Father is holy, divine love should not be sentimentalized and traded upon for our selfish ends. God is not an easy-going parent, a "soft touch." The Father, so full of love, is also "in heaven," thus deserving our reverence and adoration, awe and wonder. The Father combines holiness and love, both the will and the power to save. Where can we see proof of this great truth? Well, remember what Jesus said: "Anyone who has seen me has seen the Father" (John 14:9).

So let us always pray mindful of the holiness of God, "the power which moves in love, and the love which has behind it the undefeatable power of God."[16] At the same time, Bible translators point out that the Aramaic term *abba* which begins the Lord's Prayer should be rendered in English as "Dear Father," even "Dearest Father." Either of these phrases "captures both the warm confidence and the deep reverence that we have for our Father in heaven."[17]

One other thing must be remembered. Jews were always conscious of being the chosen people of God. A persistent theme of the Hebrew Scriptures is this fact, so basic and precious, and so likely to prompt a sense of arrogant exclusiveness. Jews were tempted to say, "We are God's special people and you are not!" Jesus certainly celebrated the gracious chosenness of his ethnic people, but he also repudiated the idea that God has favorites to the exclusion of others. None are deserving. We all are chosen if and when we decide to accept God's gracious choice of us.

When we accept the high privilege of being God's chosen people, we are sent on mission for the salvation of others, not consumed with the awareness of how special we are as handpicked children of God. People build dividing walls—"I'm inside, you're outside"—but God tears them down. Therefore, in Christ there is no more Jew or

16. Barclay, *Lord's Prayer*, 21.

17. Ryken, *Prayer of Our Lord*, 23.

Gentile, male or female, but unity among all who accept God as their Father and thus are connected with each other in God's family.

We hear this in the opening and closing verses of Psalm 8, which are identical: "O Lord, our Sovereign, how majestic is your name in all the earth!" God cannot be privatized, no matter how much we are tempted to feel we have some special access or personal corner on the divine. In giving his disciples this Prayer, Jesus refused to cut them off from the larger family of God. The *our* of "our Father" is love responding to love, which then leads to loving relationships that embrace the whole community of faith and the mission of the Son in and through that community, the church.

The One "in heaven," the invisible who has now become most visible in Jesus Christ, is reverenced in the first words of the Lord's Prayer. It spells death to human "isms" that divide when God does not—nationalisms, racisms, classisms, and the ugly rest. The Holy One is gathering a family of equals. All its members are undeserving and yet reborn by divine grace. And all people are invited to join in this miraculous rebirth.

"Hallowed" Be Your Name

"Hallowed be your name" is to be our express intent for God, says Jesus. "Hallowed" draws upon the Greek *hagios* (holy), essentially meaning "different from other things." God's name is different from other names. It is not to be "taken in vain," used glibly, selfishly, harshly, to no effect. To hallow God's name goes beyond being respectful of it, or showing reverence for it. Hallowing the divine Name involves actual transformation of the one who hallows it. The one praying must become what the name implies and makes possible. She or he must do with courage what that special name calls forth. In Hebrew, each person's name indicated that individual's nature, character, or special trait. So our prayer to let God's name be "hallowed" means that we gladly grant to God the unique place that his nature and character and actions deserve and demand in our lives.

Abraham Lincoln, in his famous Gettysburg Address, used the word *hallow*, which we seldom hear our national leaders utter these days. He said, "In a larger sense we cannot dedicate, we cannot consecrate, we cannot hallow this ground." The blood of those who had fought and died there had already set Gettysburg apart from all other places, better than any words could. And now the Son of God, through the shedding of his blood, has shown us the Father's heart, character, and gracious intent in a way we could never have seen otherwise. He sacrificial death has hallowed the Father's love.

The most familiar current use of the word *hallow* is in a weird holiday we call Halloween, which originally was "All Hallows' Evening," the night before the church's celebration of All Saints' Day. Once a sacred day on the church calendar, it has been transformed by an unbelieving society into something very different—a night to shiver at shadows and scream at ghosts. What All Saints' Day once was, Christian prayer and worship always should be, declare anew the ancient words of Psalm 8:1. "O Lord, our Sovereign, how majestic is your name in all the earth!"

We must never forget this. Prayer inspired by the divine majesty has life-changing implications for the one praying. To pray "hallowed be Thy name" necessarily entails a pledge to be accountable to that name. As one writer put it, "If I pray for God's name to be treated as holy, yet have no regard for manifesting holiness in my own life, I am a hypocrite."[18] As we pray this way, we realize that we are stewards of the amazing privilege participating in the divine nature and mission (2 Peter 1:4).

Rather than opening a worship service with a folksy comment like, "Hi, friends, good to see you all today," we might better begin as Nehemiah did: "Blessed be your glorious name, which is exalted above all blessing and praise!" (Neh 9:5). Hallowing God's name is the proper way to open Christian worship and prayer. Our prayers are first to acknowledge and celebrate the holiness of God. We certainly "are not to rush into the presence of God, snap our fingers toward heaven and expect the angels to jump! We begin with proper worship."[19]

In effect, Jesus asks his praying disciples to surround all that they may affirm or ask with the spirit of Psalm 111: "Praise the

18. Kendall, *Lord's Prayer*, 83.

19. Ibid., 39.

Lord! Great are the works of the Lord, full of splendor and majesty, faithful and just. Holy and awesome is God's name!" This reverence for God is the heart of worship, the beginning of wisdom, and the beginning of the Lord's Prayer. In the words of another psalm, we may say, "Let my prayer be counted as incense before you, and the lifting up of my hands as an evening sacrifice" (Ps 141:2).

Becoming aware of God's transcendence is a difficult and even dangerous process. The Roman Empire was collapsing in AD 410 when Augustine wrote his classic *The City of God*. He encouraged despairing Romans to fix their eyes on the heavens, beyond the painful politics of this passing world. He reminded them that the invisible is always with us—underneath, beyond, undergirding, and outlasting our evaporating empires.

Seeing by faith the heavenly Majesty can inspire and sustain us in the meantime. We should fix our eyes on Jesus (Heb 12:22). Lying just beyond our natural vision is a spiritual world. Jesus calls attention to the enduring reality of God "in heaven," to the simultaneous reality of the physical and the spiritual, to the urgent need for his disciples to look beyond the despair of the moment to that Truth that unaided human eyes cannot see.

The psalmist asked God two humbling and yet hopeful questions. "Where can I go from your Spirit? Or where can I flee from your presence?" (139:7). The obvious answer to both questions is, Nowhere! What, then, is true holiness for followers of Jesus? It is a life-reshaping reverence. It is seeing and submitting to the invisible spiritual reality of God in the heavens as real reverence. Holiness is the outcome of a life that truly sees and properly submits to the eternal God.

Seeing the divine presence, however, is particularly difficult when our lives are driven by an endless flood of activity. We must be still in order to know that he is God (Ps 46:10). As Psalm 65 declares, "Silence is praise to you, Zion-dwelling God, and also obedience. You hear the prayer in it all" (MSG).

The constant flow of emails, electronic texts, television specials, urgent appointments, and new worlds to visit and conquer distract us from the fact that our lives are being lived on very thin ice. Our lives are so full, our eyes so cluttered, and our ears so plugged that our awareness of spiritual reality is overwhelmed. Our vision of God fades into the darkness of nothingness.

To hallow God's name, we must be still, look beyond our pressing daily priorities, and allow ourselves to be shaped by "the Other." We must pursue holiness—that is, recognize the holiness of God and seek to reflect it in some small measure. The life of holiness is the great reversal of what is backward, the ultimate medicine for the sickness of sin, turning back and daring to face life again. The pervasive malady of our day is ADHD (Attention Deficit Hyperactivity Disorder), but we might call the pursuit of holiness a radically different kind of ADHD (Alternate Direction that Hallows the Divine). It's a break with the usual, a choice to live the opposite of the common routine (Gk., *koinos*). It is to be intentionally open to God's way of life, which is quite different from the common run of things.

Early Christians were sometimes called "saints"—the holy ones, the ones set apart for God, those who are sanctified (Acts 20:32). They knew that hallowing is a disciple's proper stance toward God. Only then will God graciously set us aside and set us on a glorious path of Godlike difference. Hallowing God's name means that we create a context of reverence in which we ask God to be honored by the new way we live. We hallow him with words of adoration and lives of surrender and obedience. We hallow God by reflecting the divine character in the practicalities of our existence, by living the uncommon life in the midst of the common.

The New Testament Greek word for *saints* comes from the same root word as the verb meaning "to hallow." This suggests that as we hallow God's name, he hallows us. God answers the first petition of the Lord's Prayer by sanctifying those who pray, making them saints. Our baptism as believers is an act that bears witness to the holiness of God's name. At the same time, our baptism announces that now we are traveling the holiness path by God's grace. This is why we are baptized in the name of the Father, the Son, and the Holy Spirit (Matt 28:19; 1 Cor 6:11). So, "now that God has placed his name on us, he is known to be holy whenever we are holy...If we bear the name 'Christian,' we must become what we are: set apart for God in purity. We *are* holy because of what Jesus Christ has done *for* us. But we must continue to *be* holy by what his Spirit does *in* us."[20]

The Pursuit of Holiness

Recognizing and celebrating God's holiness leads us to have that holiness reflected in ourselves. But there is natural resistance to this greatest of all human privileges and goals. The reasons for avoiding the pursuit of holiness are many.

The very idea of a holy life seems archaic and elitist, an outdated Puritan ideal, an impossible dream of perfection, a legalistic quagmire, a relic of medieval monasticism, a sign of someone just wanting to be better in appearance than in fact they are. Isn't holiness for religious professionals, the prerogative of affluent people who have time and resources that allow them to focus on the "nice" things of life? Haven't you seen those disgraced ministers and priests on the news? Aren't we just asking for trouble when we claim to be Christlike? Besides, who wants to be a marginalized prude?

On and on go the questions. But the call of the Lord's Prayer also goes on and on. Christ calls us to resist the usual holiness questions and determine to reverence God's name. In the process, we will be hallowed by God. The seductions and failures are there, of course, but so is the transforming grace of God.

Recall the biblical challenge and warning: "Pursue peace with everyone, and the holiness without which no one will see the Lord" (Heb 12:14). David Timms says it well: "In hallowing His name, we acknowledge that His holiness enables our fulfillment...When we hallow His name, he confronts everything destructive and poisonous within us...Indeed, what we declare of Him He desires for us, precisely."[21]

Sin is to insist on doing *my* things *my* way for *my* own pleasure and *by myself*, apart from God—even in defiance of God, and even if it leads to my own destruction. Humans were created to live in loving relationship with God. To honor the "I" instead of honoring God

20. Ryken, *Prayer of Our Lord*, 31, 32.

21. Timms, *Living the Lord's Prayer*, 94, 95.

destroys one's very being and future. The Lord's Prayer is the utter opposite of such an individualistic rebuke thrown in the face of God.

You cannot pray the Lord's Prayer
And even once say "I."
You cannot say the Lord's Prayer
And even once say "My."
Nor can you pray the Lord's Prayer
And not pray for another,
For when you ask for daily bread
You must include your brother.
For others are included
In each and every plea—
From the beginning to the end of it,
It never once says "Me!"[22]

Being made new in God's image is the only way to become the persons God created us to be.

As we noted at the outset, the Lord's Prayer directs our attention both to God as "Father" and to God "in heaven." The first speaks of God's nearness to us and love of us. That should amaze and melt our hearts. The second speaks of God's distance from and difference from us. The technical terms are *immanence* (God is near) and *transcendence* (God is above, beyond, wholly other). The prophet Isaiah describes beautifully this important balance of nearness and beyondness (57:15). He quotes the God who dwells in the holy place, very different from where we dwell, who also chooses to be with us right where we are.

> For thus says the high and lofty one who inhabits eternity, whose name is Holy: "I dwell in the high and holy place, and also with those who are contrite and humble in spirit, to revive the spirit of the humble, and to revive the heart of the contrite."

22. Zodhiates, *Lord's Prayer*, 7.

The Lord's Prayer celebrates the fact that the transcendent One in heaven has arrived in Jesus as the immanent Father, right in the middle of our earthly lives. To pray properly is to drop to one's knees in amazement and adoration of the heavenly One; it also is to rise to our feet to be fully and warmly embraced by that same One who has chosen to walk with us throughout this life and forever.

Discussion Guide

1. Dr. Callen writes that "prayer inspired by the divine majesty has life-changing implications for the one praying." Recall a prayer time when you were impressed by the majesty of God. How did that experience affect you?
2. How would you describe the relationship between the divine Father, Son, and Holy Spirit? What does the doctrine of the Trinity reveal about what happens when we pray?
3. This chapter speaks of essential "twin realities" about God that too often are separated in church life. What are they? How are both expressed in the worship services of the church you attend?
4. Is your life so busy, your agenda so full, that being still and communing with God is a virtual impossibility? What if anything is truly important on your to-do list for today?
5. Does God ever seem so far away that you wonder whether your prayers move him? Can you think of anyone Jesus met during his earthly ministry who felt the same way? How did Jesus convince them of the immanence of God (i.e., that God is involved in our daily lives)?

The "Pater Noster"

The Lord's prayer has been loved and prayed by all generations of Christians. For many centuries, the prayer was prayed in Latin.

PATER noster, qui es in cœlis;
sanctificatur nomen tuum:
Adveniat regnum tuum;
fiat voluntas tua, sicut in cœlo, et in terra.
Panem nostrum cotidianum da nobis hodie:
Et dimitte nobis debita nostra,
sicut et nos dimittimus debitoribus nostris:
et ne nos inducas in tentationem:
sed libera nos a malo.

[to which may be added]:
Quia tuum est regnum, et potestas, et Gloria,
in saecula.
Amen.

CHAPTER 4
Thy Kingdom Come

How amazing that communication is possible with none other than the Lord God Almighty! From the heart of such communication, we say to ourselves, "If only we could become holy as God is holy—not sinful like the world we're in, but reflective of the purity that we experience when we're in God's presence." God has expressed the same desire to see us become like him (Lev 11:45), but surely this is impossible.

However, Jesus encourages us to think that godliness might be possible. The Lord's Prayer turns from its God-oriented beginning to point out ways we might realize a similar kind of holiness. The apostle Paul in 1 Thessalonians 5 urges believers to live sanctified lives that are separated from sin and surrendered to the Lord (5:23–24). John observes that "all who have this hope in him [Christ] purify themselves, just as he [God] is pure" (1 John 3:3).

After recognizing and reverencing the holy God, it is entirely appropriate to ask that the complete reign of God reach every corner of our world and every layer of our individual lives as we believe and pray. The point of praying is to "learn how to conform our will to His Will."[1] We must begin with who we are, where we are, and what we do if we are to reflect God's very character and become forerunners of the coming reign of God. Yes, the kingdom is coming. One day Jesus will reign through "those who receive the abundance of grace and the free gift of righteousness" (Rom 5:17). In the

1. Day, *Lord's Prayer*, 35.

meantime, Jesus expects his disciples to reflect God's character and will, increasingly becoming agents of the coming kingdom of God.

At one point, the catechism of Martin Luther asks, "How is God's name hallowed among us?" His answer is, "When both our life and doctrine are truly Christian." In other words, when our convictions and practical actions are fully submitted to the will of God, we hallow God's name. Jesus says that we are to pray this to God: "Let your kingdom come, Let your will be done, as in heaven, so also on earth." Remember what happened to the one who said this. We who follow him must be aware that "Christianity means conflict. We never forget, as we pray, that the one who taught us to pray in this way was crucified."[2] We who believe must walk a similar path, take the same risks, enter into the same joy, and share the same destiny.

Citizens of a Kingdom

The glory days of kings are long gone. North Americans tend to be of two minds about this. We sometimes are fascinated with the pageantry that can surround the British royal family. At the same time, we are averse to the very idea of anyone holding sovereignty over a nation's citizens. Many of our ancestors died in the Revolutionary War to gain independence from the British crown. Kings and queens suggest totalitarianism, and we Americans will have none of that, thank you.

Despite our aversion to a monarchy, the will and ways of God were put in such terms in the biblical context. The concept of the "kingdom of God" ties together the Old and New Testaments. We need to understand God's reign in that biblical context before we can transfer the idea to our modern context and reapply it appropriately.

King-related words are used in two different senses in the Lord's Prayer, one denoting God's king*dom* and the other God's king*ship*. The first word points to the God of creation, the originator and thus the sovereign over all that was or will be. The second word points to the degree to which that divine sovereignty is fully operative here and now, despite our human fallenness.

2. Willimon and Hauerwas, *Lord, Teach Us*, 15.

This pair of words follows the pattern of Hebrew parallelism, where the second phrase echoes or explains the first. What is meant by "Thy kingdom come"? It is that "Thy will be done." The *kingdom* of God will become the operative *kingship* of God when God's will is shared and put into practice in this world, in and by us. God's kingdom is primarily a quality of spirit, a focus of will. In brief, "whenever a man acts in the spirit of Christ, there is the kingdom of God. And when all men everywhere learn to act in accordance with God's will, the kingdom of God will be present in its fullness."[3] In the earthly ministry of Jesus, the kingdom of God came very near. We might even say that in Jesus the kingship of God became fully visible in an actual life.

John Crossan suggests that it would be helpful to rephrase "kingdom of God" to read the "ruling style of God." He imagines how this present world would be if God chaired the corporate boards of all large businesses and was the president and prime minister of all nations of the world. It is the dream "of an earth where the Holy One of justice and righteousness actually gets to establish—as we might say—the annual budget for the global economy."[4] There would be some big changes then!

Well, where do we place our ultimate loyalty as believers? Regardless of what's printed on our passports and drivers' licenses, where is our real citizenship? Christians are no longer to belong to this world system (John 17:14–19), but "to a heavenly counterculture that is hated by the same world system that hated Jesus and crucified him."[5] When Jesus told Pilate, "My kingdom is not of this world," he did not mean that his kingdom would have to be established elsewhere. He meant that the nature of his government is *other than* the typical nature of governments in this present world.

Admittedly, if we choose to be mature citizens of God's kingdom, we have a lot of explaining to do. After all, if Jesus is the King of Kings as the Bible says, why is this world still so fragmented, fearful, and rebellious? Why is even the church, the supposed gathering

3. Day, *Lord's Prayer*, 38.

4. Crossan, *Greatest Prayer*, 78.

5. Wiersbe, *On Earth as It Is in Heaven*, 66.

of God's holy citizens, often in disarray and thwarted in its mission? Maybe it's for the same reason that ancient Israel was divided and defeated—"they rejected their heavenly King and asked for an earthly king so they could imitate the godless nations. Instead of rejoicing that they were God's unique and special people, they imitated the pagan nations and sacrificed their distinctive witness."[6]

If we accept the idea that there is a difference between God's eternal *kingdom* and his present *kingship* in the lives of those who follow him, we begin to understand more about how God chooses to work in this world. We understand how God could grant moral freedom to us creatures, and how we could misuse it, thus spoiling what otherwise would have been a world governed according to the divine ideal. In this spoiled environment, the holiness-hungry believer nonetheless longs for the fullness of God's reign here and now. So the believer prays that the kingdom of the first creation day will become the kingship of this present day. Yet it is understood that the kingdom will have to begin with God's kingship in the believer's life and then move outward into the broader society.

The text of the Lord's Prayer most commonly used today ends with glad recognition that at both the beginning and the end of time, God's kingdom will be fully present: "For yours is the kingdom and the power and the glory, forever and ever!" However, immediately before that, the Prayer asks that "Your kingdom come." The fullness of God's effective reign, which was at first and later will be, should be happening now. So we pray and work to that end.

The Kingdom Here and Now

Now here's a paradox. In order for us to pray that God's kingdom will come in our midst, we must be aware of what God's reign is. We must also be convinced that it already has come, at least in part. Otherwise, we could not make sense of the idea. It has already come, at least to some part of our lives. We are aware of the kingdom's character and potential, thanks especially to the coming of Jesus.

6. Ibid., 65.

This is exactly where Jesus' disciples were struggling. Their kingdom expectations were filled with political overtones—especially driving out the hated Romans. But Jesus, the dependable reflection of God's full reign in an earthly life, wasn't much of a guerilla leader. His ideas about kingship were unusual, to say the least. He kept talking about gaining glorious life through humble death, turning the other cheek, and loving our enemies. And he implied strongly that the kingship of God already was operative in his own life. If that really were the case, the kingdom expectations of the disciples needed some major revision.

Let's return to an important feature of Hebrew literature, *parallelism*. This is a writing technique that says something twice for emphasis or explanation, with the second repeating or clarifying the meaning of the first. The psalmist, for instance, reports that "the Lord of hosts is with us; the God of Jacob is our refuge" (Ps 46:7). The second clause both repeats and notes the fuller implication of the first clause. They stand in parallel, repetitive to a degree, but not redundant.

There is also parallelism in the Lord's Prayer: "Your kingdom come, Your will be done in earth as it is in heaven." The kingdom of God is a life or a community of lives where God's will is being accomplished on earth as in heaven. To pray for the coming of the kingdom of heaven is the same thing as to pray for our own submission to and fulfillment of the will of God here and now.

The first believers soon knew that the fullness of the divine reign had been clearly manifest in Jesus' own life (Mark 1:15). The kingdom message was central to the whole ministry of Jesus (v 14). King Jesus, unlike other kings, is his people's servant, even their sacrifice. The challenge is that the divine reign should also begin happening *in the disciples*. Jesus instructed them to realize this and pray that it might be so. They were to pray that the holiness recognized in Jesus would be realized in themselves. Yet they could not expect to achieve this holy life of themselves, but somehow through him.

Contrary to the thinking of power-oriented believers in the first and twenty-first centuries, God's kingdom is not a nation, empire, or ethnic group seeking dominance. God's kingdom includes Jews, for instance, but the people known as Jews are not automatically citizens of the kingdom (Rom 2:28–29). The kingdom has no secret rites and privileges available only to the lucky few who are "predestined." It is not an institution, not even a church. The kingdom is God's way of seeing and doing things, the actual reign of Jesus Christ in our lives and in our world.

The kingdom of God is "less concerned about orthodoxy than about conversion, justice, and compassion."[7] As a kingdom person, a citizen of God's arriving reign, a humble believer is not "a physical unit in a religious organization. I'm a living part of a miraculous spiritual unity in Christ—a member of one body (1 Cor 12:12–14), a stone in one temple (Eph 2:19–22; 1 Peter 2:4–7), a branch in one vine (John 15:1–9), to name but a few of the New Testament images of the church."[8]

The kingdom of God "is not a *place*, but rather a *relationship*. It exists wherever people enthrone Jesus as Lord of their lives."[9] And yet, the righting of personal relationships is not altogether adequate. Jesus came with a spiritual message of personal salvation, which involves the righting of the relationship between individuals and their God. Still, God's kingdom is to come on earth as it is in heaven. It is to come in a space-time world that is not one-dimensional (personal or social, political or nonpolitical). It involves the release of individuals from sin as well as healing for the nations.

Jesus was the incarnation (enfleshment) of God, the kingdom realized. His disciples are to be in him in such a comprehensive way that they perpetuate the enfleshment of God in and for the fallen world. We disciples, in other words, are to continue praying and enacting the Lord's prayer—enfleshed spirituality, holistic holiness. One writer uses an interesting musical analogy for this: "Jesus is the musical genius who wrote the greatest oratorio of all time; we are the musicians, captivated by his composition ourselves, who now perform it before a world full of Muzak and cacophony."[10]

7. Gafney, *Guide to the "Our Father" Today*, 38.

8. Wiersbe, *On Earth as It Is in Heaven*, 41.

9. Packer, *Praying the Lord's Prayer*, 50.

10. Wright, *Lord and His Prayer*, 30.

Praying Jesus-style births in us a radical holiness, personal and social, marked by *conversion* and *subversion*, a transformation of people and their societies into the likeness of Christ. The Christian mission is to live like Christ so that redeeming love might upset the strongholds of evil in us and in the world around us. To the degree that these strongholds are upset, God's kingship has come.

The Kingdom Universal

The God of Israel is the Holy One whom Jews address in prayers as "king of the universe." Jesus announced again this great reality but altered the expected nature of the divine kingdom that people are to enter. The kingdom Jesus had in view was not Israel reestablished as a political and geographic entity, but something much larger. God's dominion would cover not only the "Holy Land," but all land, indeed the whole earth. The basic means of making God's future our present, God's royal eternity a currently reigning reality, was expressed in a prayer of Jesus near the end of his earthly life: "My Father, if it is possible, let this cup pass from me; yet not what I want but what you want" (Matt 26:39).

In this Gethsemane prayer and the Lord's Prayer we begin to see the real character of Christian holiness. "Every word of the Lord's Prayer reflects the Lord's vision of what our lives should be—unified, all-embracing response to the love of our heavenly Father, so that we seek his glory, trust his care, and obey his word every moment of every day."[11] The God whose very name we hallow is the God whose will we must obey. To so hallow and obey is to be holy in the eyes of God.

We who carry the name *Christian* are called to a prayerful renouncing of a selfish orientation of life. We are directed to reject every citizenship that assumes priority over God's reign. We are to seek the active reign of God in all aspects of our lives. And our acknowledgment of this divine reign is not to be a grudging concession, but a gripping and life-producing affirmation. We are to "become so enthralled with a vision of what God is doing on earth

11. Packer, *Praying the Lord's Prayer*, 57.

and in heaven that we forget the story that the world has told us—that we have nothing better to do than to satisfy our desires"—and we will recognize as false and sinful the lure of our culture that presents itself as "a vast supermarket of desire in which we are encouraged constantly to consume."[12]

When they heard this Prayer, the first twelve disciples of Jesus were just beginning to understand that God's will has been done on earth. Jesus is our pioneer, our inspiration, our resource in the journey of faith. The crossroads of history were formed by crossbars of rough wood where the clash of wills, human and divine, hung openly, horribly, with the powers and principalities of this world finally exposed and conquered. The ministry keynote of Jesus was the realized kingdom, the full and present reign of God. That past emphasis of his must now become our present.

Jürgen Moltmann has put it well: "Anyone who gets involved with Jesus gets involved with the kingdom of God...Anyone who looks for God and asks about the kingdom in which 'righteousness and peace will kiss each other' (Ps 85:10) should look at Jesus and enter into the things that happened in his presence and that still happen today in his Spirit. That is obviously and palpably true; for who is Jesus? Simply *the kingdom of God in person.*"[13]

Who is invited into this kingdom of Jesus? Its potential membership highlights how radical and upsetting is the vision of Jesus, how different from the common expectation of his time or ours. Jesus invited people into a kingdom of love that is open to all people! Look at the group Jesus collected as his first disciples—decent God-fearing fishermen; a despised tax collector; an insurrectionist Zealot or two. In the larger circle of his followers, we see disgraced women of the village, the poor, even lepers and disturbed lunatics lurking among the tombs. This was going to be a different kind of kingdom!

This kingdom of God involves a great diversity that nonetheless is bound tightly together by the miracle of God's love. A few lines by John Fawcett capture the miraculous potential of this divine kingdom:

12. Willimon and Hauerwas, *Lord, Teach Us*, 66.

13. Moltmann, *Jesus Christ for Today's World*, 7.

Blest be the tie that binds
Our hearts in Christian love:
The fellowship of kindred minds
Is like to that above.

Unfortunately, a sad bit of doggerel states what too often is the actual case in church life:

To live above with saints we love,
Will certainly be glory.
To live below with saints we know—
Well, that's another story.

That alternate version raises some uncomfortable questions. Has the glory of God departed from some of our homes, churches, and church ministries? Do we go on with our business as usual and hardly miss God's departure? Is there really glory in the church or just crowds of people seeking a little relief from the meaningless routines of life, perhaps with a bit of wholesome entertainment?

The Kingdom in Daily Practice

We find an important indication of what Christ expected of our church life when we look at the overall structure of the Lord's Prayer. The literary device of parallelism does not always appear in successive lines of a biblical text. In the Lord's Prayer, for example, two *sections* parallel each other, the second reflecting and detailing the proper fulfillment of the first. God's "name…kingdom…will," when rightly hallowed, form a discipleship that rightly handles the practical matters of "bread…debts…temptations."

These two sections belong to each other, mirror each other, and depend on each other. To separate them is to ruin everything. The Lord's Prayer sends us into the world with clear priorities and an awareness that all begins and ends with the holy God, to whom the ultimate victory belongs. Such a view of reality as a whole should bring tears to our humbled eyes and strength to our growing faith. If we pretend to hallow God's name and fail to practice loving justice, our religion is merely a self-defeating lie. On the other hand, if we kneel in wonder before the holy God, we will have our necessary bread, forgiveness of debts, and deliverance from temptation.

The Hebrew prophets often cite a contradiction between carrying on ritual prayer and failing to enact righteous justice. To speak holy words and live unholy lives is a more serious matter than breaking the rules of biblical parallelism. It is blaspheming a holy God! God calls for the kind of prayer that leads to holy living. Any kind of prayer that leads elsewhere, or nowhere, falls under divine judgment. Says God, "For I desire steadfast love and not sacrifice [empty prayer words], the knowledge of God rather than burnt offerings" (Hos 6:6). God's instruction "there" must be our instruction "here," God's "then" in Jesus is our "now" of living in Christ's Spirit. Anything other is disastrous for the Christian witness in the world.

An American businessman once said to Brennan Manning: "At our annual shareholders meeting in Las Vegas each year, the sexual behavior of Christians is no different from that of unbelievers. And why not? Everybody has a good time and nobody gets hurt."[14] Manning reacted vigorously to this sad report, insisting that such behavior on the part of Christians is absolutely intolerable.

The church, in Las Vegas or anywhere else, is to be "the living extension of Jesus Christ in time and space."[15] Paul's word to the Galatians may sound like utter folly to modern secular culture, but it is the nonnegotiable standard for serious Christian believers: "May I never boast of anything except the cross of our Lord Jesus Christ, by which the world has been crucified to me and I to the world" (Gal 6:14). That sacred death leads to resurrection life.

To honestly pray "Thy kingdom come" is to cry out for our own experience of the holiness of God; it is to declare our willingness to participate in God's kingdom that is coming. We want it to come first in us and then for all others. It's hard for us to realize how extremely difficult it must have been for the Twelve to accept the dramatic fact that God's kingdom was already arriving in Jesus. Had they dared, they might have asked Jesus, "Where exactly is this

14. Manning, *Signature of Jesus*, 79.

15. Ibid., 84.

transformed world you speak of?" Tiberius was still the corrupt emperor in Rome, Antipas still the lecherous tetrarch of Galilee, and Pilate the vacillating prefect of Judea. The poor were still poor and the injustices of imperial domination were unchanged. "So how has the kingdom come in you?" they may well have asked. Can you imagine Jesus' answer?

John Crossan has tried to imagine it this way: "You have been waiting for God, while God has been waiting *for you*. No wonder nothing is happening. You want God's intervention, while God wants your *collaboration*. God's kingdom is here, but only insofar as you accept it, enter it, live it, and thereby establish it."[16] Our cooperation with God is essential. When we do choose to act as agents of God's Spirit, we must keep one thing clearly in mind: The divine kingdom comes *through* us, but never wholly *by* us. The kingdom is always God's!

As the Lord's Prayer concludes, it declares that the kingdom initiative—the enabling grace, the real power, and the ultimate glory—are God's, not ours. Even so, God seeks responsible partners and co-laborers in covenant with him. Our salvation is by grace alone, but that divine grace cannot remain ours alone. Once received, it is gladly embodied and shared with others in great need.

Jesus said, rather shockingly, "Love your enemies and pray for those who persecute you" (Matt 5:44). The difference between Jesus and Pilate was that the life of one flowed from God and was rooted in self-giving love, while the other's was mired in self-seeking greed, personal power, and self-preservation, none of which came from God. One was embracing life redemptively; the other was grabbing it as violently as necessary. So the Lord's Prayer is less about God's kingdom coming someday to destroy all our enemies, and more about the empowerment of disciples like us who are prepared to assist God in inaugurating the kingdom today!

16. Crossan, *Greatest Prayer*, 89–90.

Kingdom Metaphors

Metaphors for such a kingdom's arrival are many, and sometimes graphically misleading. One evangelist proclaimed this to a camp meeting congregation: "Come! Put your all on the altar and die! Then the kingdom of God will have come to you, right here and right now." That kind of emotional call would certainly frighten the person not acquainted with common holiness language of two or three generations ago, just as the language of the earliest Christians was sometimes misunderstood by "outsiders." The believers said that they gathered to "eat the flesh and drink the blood" of their Savior. Out of context, such words were frightening, although they carry good biblical meaning.

The apostle Paul announced with thanksgiving that he had been "crucified with Christ" and no longer was alive. He said it was "Christ who lives in me" (Gal 2:20). Indeed, holiness in one sense is death, the releasing of control over our lives—although we actually have far less control than we like to think. How hard it is to yield, to be a child again, to trust fully in another, even if the other is God. But to such trusting children belongs the kingdom of God!

Here is another metaphor for holiness, which may sound quaint to today's urban dwellers, but which is still understandable and appropriate. David Liverett is an artist who once developed a fascination with barns—old barns, round barns, all kinds and conditions of barns. He traveled the countryside photographing those of most visual interest and then drew illustrations of them in a wonderful pointillism style. Finally, and with accompanying commentary by a range of his friends, there came the 2006 book *Light from the Barn*. David's passion, however, was for more than mere barns. It was nostalgia combined with spiritual meditation, which was almost poetic at points.

Likewise, Jesus turned to the barns of his day for a vivid spiritual lesson about kingdom building. Farmers in Jesus' day often built bigger and bigger barns to hoard their growing stores of grain. Jesus pointed to the foolishness of such personal kingdom building (Luke 12:18), because our time on earth is short. Others need our surplus. We will be held accountable, and maybe sooner than expected!

Can't we move away from our all-too-human tendency to fabricate our own security and success through the accumulation of titles, power positions, financial assets, houses and barns, condos, and mutual fund accounts?

Notice that the Lord's Prayer in Matthew appears at the end of the Sermon on the Mount, the blueprint given by Jesus for a new way to be and live in this world. We are to "strive first for God's kingdom and his righteousness" (Matt 6:33). As one bumper sticker wisely says, "Tithe if you love Jesus. Anyone can honk!" We must put our actions where our affirmations are.

Accepting God's Reign

To be "holy" is to accept the reign of God in one's own life. According to Jesus, such an acceptance involves repenting that leads to baptism (Matt 3:2; 4:17), becoming like a little child (Mark 10:15), putting one's abilities and resources to work for godly purposes (Matt 25:14–30), striving to enter the kingdom of God (Luke 13:24), seeking to be "perfect" as God is perfect (Matt 5:48), and knowing firsthand "the power of his resurrection" (Phil 3:8–10).

Such an acceptance of God's reign was reflected well by John Wesley in a marvelous prayer of self-surrender:

> I am no longer my own, but yours. Put me to what you will, rank me with whom you will; put me to doing, put me to suffering; let me be employed for you or laid aside for you, exalted for you or brought low for you; let me be full, let me be empty; let me have all things, let me have nothing; I freely and wholeheartedly yield all things to your pleasure and disposal.[17]

Praying that way is inviting the kingdom of God to come in our hearts and in our time.

17. As quoted in Ryken, *Prayer of Our Lord*, 52–53.

Discussion Guide

1. What do you mean when you speak of "kingdom of God"? Is it of this world or not? Is it to be seen now or only later?

2. How could Christians insist with Jesus that the kingdom of God has come, when so little seems to have changed in this sinful world?

3. Have you ever "died" to yourself—that is, truly yielded your will to the will of the holy God for you? Would you do it now?

4. What would it mean in your own life if you tore down all your barns of selfish hoarding to share the power of Christ's resurrection with others, like a trusting little child?

5. Recall those four lines of doggerel in this chapter that speak of the difficulty of living with the "saints we know." Do we you think we have a holiness problem in the church today? If so, how can it be changed?

The Lord's Prayer

Our Father in heaven, hallowed be your name.
Your kingdom come.
Your will be done, on earth as it is in heaven.
Give us this day our daily bread.
And forgive us our debts, as we also have forgiven our debtors.
And do not bring us to the time of trial, but rescue us from the evil one.
—Matthew 6:9-13 NRSV

CHAPTER 5

Give Us This Day

As we saw in the previous chapter, the Lord's Prayer has two parallel sections, one dealing with spiritual concerns and the other with practical, mundane issues. We now look more closely at section two.

The priority sequence of Christian prayer has been established. God is holy and we are to hallow that divine wonder. Then comes what should be the natural consequence of that awareness, including our practical requests. The sequence is stated well by Babbie Mason in her song "With All My Heart" when she prays, "Help me, Lord, to seek Your face before I seek Your hand."

It is somewhat like a father coming home from a long business trip. His children run to him, saying, "Daddy, what did you bring us?" After some loving instruction by their mother, a later return is greeted with, "Oh Daddy, we've missed you so much and are so glad to see you again!" He receives their love and soon reveals that he has brought some wonderful gifts. It's a matter of putting first things first, not one or the other, but both in the proper sequence of priority. Disciples of Jesus are to rejoice and adore, hallow and submit to God, simply and honestly as the Father God is encountered.

The pattern of the Lord's Prayer follows Jesus' own Jewish heritage. It repeats the pattern of the Ten Commandments, where the first four focus on the proper view of and relationship with God, and the rest instruct us in proper paths of living. "I am the Lord, your God," announces the divine. Because he has done great things for us, there are certain ways we are to live in this world in response to his graciousness (Ex 20:2). Similarly, Jesus moves from the first three petitions (God's name be hallowed, God's kingdom come, God's will be done) to the final three petitions of the Lord's Prayer (getting bread, finding forgiveness, avoiding temptation).

The "Therefore" Pivot

With the whole of God's being, purposes, and provisions in view, we bring to God's feet the whole of our earthly lives. First, we are to worship God and seek God's kingdom and righteousness; then "all these things will be given to you as well" (Matt 6:33). The overall pattern of the Lord's prayer is:

The THY petitions:
Thy name be honored
Thy kingdom come
Thy will be done

The PIVOT:
On earth as it is in heaven

The US petitions:
Give us bread
Forgive our debts
Lead us not into temptation
Deliver us from evil.

We now are in the middle and at the heart of the Lord's Prayer. Before the pivot, we praise the holiness of God ("Hallowed be Thy name"), embrace the purpose of God ("Thy kingdom come"), and commit ourselves to the plan of God ("Thy will be done"). After the pivot we ask for the provision of God ("Give us our daily bread"), the pardon of God ("Forgive us our debts"), the power of God ("Lead us not into temptation"), and the protection of God ("Deliver us from the evil one")The very structure of the Prayer emphasizes that prayer is a partnership between God and his faithful children. Humbled, we believers reach to our heavenly Father, first in adoration and then in petition. God reaches back with the answers and gifts that we need to accomplish the divine will on earth as it is in heaven. This prayerful partnership is crucial. This is why the apostolic church put first on its agenda "prayer and the ministry of the word" (Acts 6:4). So should the church of all times and places. Only the vision of a holy God can inspire a holy life; and a holy life is partnership with the holy God for the doing of God's will. In this partnership, God offers all necessary provisions for sustaining and equipping us for ministry and mission.

"Hallowed be your name" precedes and leads to "your will be done." First we worship; then we serve. In fact, out of the worship flow the needed resources for effective service. Before Isaiah announced to God, "Here am I. Send me!" (Isaiah 6), he had been overwhelmed by a vision of the holy God. Likewise, in the New Testament there is an important linkage between Romans 11:33–36 and Romans 12:1–2. "For from him [God] and through him and to him are all things. To him be the glory forever! Amen. *Therefore*, I urge you, brothers and sisters, in view of God's mercy, to offer your bodies as a living sacrifice, holy and pleasing to God—this is true worship" (my italics). The "therefore" links part one and part two of Paul's exhortation, analogous to the two sections of the Lord's Prayer—the vision of God linked with the whole of the Christian life.

Only when God is clearly at the center of our concern and the full focus of our adoration should we move on to pray for our own personal needs. After all, true prayer is more about God than about us. The point of prayer is less to tell God what we want and much more to hear from God what we really need. It is not approaching God with our demands, but listening with our minds and hearts for God's commands.

Yet we do have real needs. These needs, according to Jesus, are three in number, covering all of time. They are (1) for present *bread*, (2) for *forgiveness* of our wayward past, and (3) for *deliverance* in order that we might approach the future successfully. These three needs are answered by the Triune nature of God. The Father is the Creator and Sustainer of all life. The Son is the Redeemer of all sin. The Spirit is God always with us to protect, guide, comfort, and finally lead us through all future days to our eternal home. The disciples of Jesus weren't seeing all of that, at least not yet; nevertheless, Jesus was equipping them to pray rightly so that they finally would.

The first petition related to our human need is to ask for daily bread. For most of us in the West today, the nearby grocery stores are full and reasonably priced. Fast-food places dot the roads of our communities. Food is not a problem, thank you. Thank who? We do our own shopping with money that we have earned, and we have made the trip ourselves. Rather than cry out for needed bread, we make ourselves sick from eating far too much of it! For many others in our world, however, survival depends on finding food each day. They are much more aware that their food is a daily gift from God, like those Hebrews of old who nearly starved in the wilderness except for the "bread" that rained down from heaven (Ex 16:1–36).

This petition of the Lord's Prayer appears simple and direct, at first glance. But there is more to it than meets the modern eye.

Bread and Ministry

In the ancient Near East, "bread" often referred to food in general. Bread was the staff of life around the Sea of Galilee, where Jesus carried on much of his ministry. Can you see in your mind's eye Galilean fishermen going off to their work in the morning with flat bread in their pockets, folded and filled with olives, cheese, and maybe figs? "The bread was both the lunch and the lunch box. It helped to make it possible for people to earn a living."[1] Jesus made it clear that prayer and stewardship, bread and ministry, must never be separated. The good creation of God provides everything needed for sustaining life and serving the Lord—that is, unless it is wasted, hoarded, or otherwise ruined.

Christ's disciples are sustained by God for the well-being of others. This is why God opens his hand "and satisfies the desires of every living thing" (Ps 145:16). Disciples, given bread by God, are to pass some of it on to satisfy the need of others. We are to eat sensibly and always give thanks. We are to be stewards more than consumers.

1. Wiersbe, *On Earth as It Is in Heaven*, 92.

Like those Jews who heard Jesus use the phrase "daily bread," we should think of the manna that fell from heaven as did those freed slaves who wandered in the wilderness, hungry and helpless except for their God (Ex 16). The Hebrew word *manna* means "What is it?" The wanderers soon learned what it was. It was God's gracious provision for their need!

Jesus compared himself to manna—"I am the bread of life" (John 6:35, 48), the "living bread from heaven" (v 51), God's ultimate provision for now and eternity. So Christians are not called to be *providers*, but *distributors*. We are bread and grace spreaders in the world—and we are to know that both are sheer gifts of God, to us as well as to others.

There is good reason to believe that, at the time of Jesus, the city of Tiberius was being developed on the western shore of the Sea of Galilee to gather more taxes and goods from the area for the increased benefit of Rome and its local administrators. This was at the expense of the Galilean people who were already poor, of course. Jesus was well aware of this. He spoke often of fish, bread, and the poor. He knew well Psalm 24:1, which says, "The earth is the Lord's and all that is in it." Seeing the local injustice by a food-controlling dictatorship, he must have thought much about who really owned the lake and all the fish in it. His conclusion?

Recall that great story recorded in John 21:2–11. The disciples are pictured as greatly frustrated because they were unable to catch any fish in the Sea of Galilee. Then Jesus directs them to a net-bursting catch. What a picture of provision and ownership, or lack thereof. We are shown dramatically that "Jesus and not Antipas is in control of the lake. It is no longer the Sea of Tiberias; it has become the Sea of Jesus!"[2]

Some have thought this shifting of Jesus from the heights of the glorious and holy God in the Prayer's first half to mere food and drink in the second half as a low-grade form of prayer. They are wrong. It is a genuine and proper progression from the earlier elements of the Lord's Prayer to this bread request. If we are to hallow God's name

2. Crossan, *Greatest Prayer*, 131.

and do his will in this broken world, we will need the strength and energy to do so. We will need bread, which is given only by God.

There's a big difference between worshiping our bodies, doing all possible to maintain our youthful appearance and enhance our physical beauty, and valuing and caring for our bodies as precious gifts of God over which we are stewards for the sake of God's coming kingdom. Beyond the strength needed by disciples, there is the stewardship issue of this request for "daily bread." All good things come from God's hand; they also come from a heart of divine love *for the benefit of all people.* Justice, including efficient food production and equitable distribution, is a critical part of the Christian gospel and calling.

One problem with so many of us is that we get to this bread-asking in the Prayer before Jesus wants us to. We easily slide over the hallowing of the name of a holy God, and the renewal of our commitment to put God's will before our own, so we can present him with our personal shopping lists of needs and wants. We "let greed get in the way of grace."[3] But the feast of bread has several dimensions of meaning in the Bible. We must not settle for the physical crumbs when a spiritual feast is being set before us!

If we suppose that holiness (God's or ours) is just some mystical something or other, only present in the heavenly realm, this bread petition should dispel our confusion. Christian holiness is anchored in the practicalities of this world. Jesus calls us to live in the present. Bread for the day is a human necessity. Jesus knew that the life of the spirit is intimately connected to the life of the body. His Jewish tradition celebrated a close and vital link between prayer and eating.

The spiritual and physical are not separate categories. Separating body and "soul" is wrong. Doesn't true worship of a loving God send us on a loving mission? Don't acts of compassion for the hungry express true worship? We should remember that one of the first teachings that spread in the early church, but was soon judged a *heresy*, claimed that a holy God could not have appeared in our foul flesh. The heretical theologians supposed that holiness and real bodies cannot mix. They said Jesus was here, yes, but not in a real body.

3. Wright, *Lord and His Prayer*, 36.

His body only seemed to be ordinary flesh. Such thinking was and remains a heresy. We must not assume that genuine holiness is impossible in this world. With God, nothing that corresponds to his will is impossible!

The most important words in the bread petition may be the *us* and *our*. We are to ask God for daily bread that is intended to be *ours*. It's not *my* bread, but a corporate gift from God. Consequently, "it is to be used, not for the benefit of the few, but for the benefit of all… If someone is starving today in India, for example, it surely is not due to God's lack of generosity but primarily to man's selfishness and secondarily to his stupidity…Hence, if we repeat the prayer 'give us this day our daily bread' and are conscious of people in need of bread and have done nothing to aid them, our prayer is a mockery."[4]

In the time of Jesus, all members of the Jewish family shared meals together. Around the table, they consciously maintained contact with God with prescribed prayers, scripture readings, and blessings. Sabbath meals, particularly the Passover meal, were heavy with memory and symbolism, recalling God's great works for his people. Therefore, "the solidarity of the people with one another and with God was remembered and also enacted in the meals."[5] Today, with the lack of intentional ritual around most tables (often with family members not there anyway), the sharing of faith from generation to generation is in serious jeopardy.

Beyond the words for *us* and *our*, notice that the petition is made in the present tense. At this point, Luke's account adds the present tense for emphasis, repeating and intensifying Matthew's account in reference to bread. Rather than saying, "Give us this day," Luke has Jesus asking that God give us "day by day." One might paraphrase this as, "Please keep feeding us as each day comes along, and then we will be able to do your will with the resulting strength available for that day." God rained down manna in the wilderness for the survival of the liberated Jews, but it could not be stored and preserved. They were dependent on God for each new day as it arrived. When Jesus sent out his disciples for their first ministry tour, he said that he was

4. Day, *Lord's Prayer*, 62.

5. Gafney, *Guide to the "Our Father" Today*, 59.

sending them with no staff, bag, bread, or money, or even a change of clothes (Luke 9:3). God would provide for them each day as they had need and were faithful journeyers on God's mission.

We are naturally curious about the future. What about saving money for vacations that rest the body for the work ahead? What about insurance and retirement planning, protecting ourselves and our families against possible financial chaos later in life? The Bible does not give specific guidelines for such things, except for one. Jesus says that where our minds and hearts are, so is our treasure. That is, if we become preoccupied with our net worth and growing portfolios, or if we become so anxious that we attempt to cover all possible eventualities, as though God were not in control of our future, we likely will be distracted from focusing on the good we could be doing today.

The Feast of God

The Bible makes a close connection between the spiritual and the physical. To the Hebrews, we humans are not bodies and souls (separate entities), but *body-souls*, fully integrated individuals. The critical incarnation—the real God with us in the real man Jesus—is the dramatic New Testament claim central to the heart of divine self-revelation. The apostle Paul applies this to everyone who would be disciples of Jesus: "Do you not know that your bodies are members of Christ himself?" (1 Cor 6:15). We are to honor our bodies as part of hallowing God's name.

Paul's application of this truth further involves a sharp critique of sexual immorality. He says that any physical union of two bodies involves a spiritual union as well. When done apart from a loving and lifelong commitment, such a union of the spiritual and physical brings a deep wrongness to the whole of one's being and to that relationship.

No Jew would have casually accused Jesus of being a "glutton and a winebibber." He was occasionally seen in the wrong places and visiting the wrong people—at least as judged by religious leaders of the time. Beyond annoyance, however, the Pharisees in particular were offended and threatened by his apparently intemperate behavior, so they deliberately spread this vicious accusation. Deuteronomy 21 described stubborn and rebellious children as gluttons and drunkards, and called for their deaths! Going well beyond reckless eating and drinking, these children were out of control, destroying their families and threatening the stability of their whole religious tradition. They deserved the worst.

So, when these accusing words were thrown at Jesus, it was because religious leaders judged that he was undermining their authority and endangering the future of the Jewish heritage. He was crossing sacred lines they had drawn, rethinking religious definitions and relationships that tended to push the recognized religious authorities off to the side. Unthinkable! Not tolerable!

When Jesus spoke to the crowds of bread and drink, he had in mind far more than ordinary foodstuffs to be chewed and swallowed. His claims were radical, seemingly almost ridiculous, and clearly blasphemous to the established religious leaders. He claimed to *be* "the bread of life" (John 6:35). Surely, he knew that God, the great and generous Father, holy and quite other, nonetheless promised that he would come near to his chosen people and "prepare a table" for them (Ps 23:5). Isaiah prophesied even more (Isa 25:6–8):

> On this mountain the Lord of hosts will make for all peoples a feast of rich food...and he will destroy on this mountain the shroud that is cast over all peoples...Then the Lord God will wipe away the tears from all faces, and the disgrace of his people he will take away from all the earth.

The Lord's Table

Today, the center of the worship life of most Christians, beyond the prayer of our Lord, is the Lord's Table. Protestants tend to celebrate it as Communion, an act of remembering the great sacrifice of Christ for us with the promise, "Do this in remembrance of me" (1 Cor 11:24). Roman Catholics have insisted that, once properly consecrated, the elements of bread and wine actually become the body and blood of Christ, newly given for us. Protestants resist this view, rejecting the theory of new sacrifice as unbiblical, unnecessary, and close to magic. They have seen how this understanding of the

Lord's Table can put into the hands of clergy too much control over the free flow of God's grace.

Our task here is not to settle this longstanding clash of views, but to make a point that clearly lies at the heart of the Lord's Prayer. We may resist concepts like *transubstantiation* (the bread's very substance becoming something else, something sacred), but we must not ignore the reality to which Jesus points. In the bread and wine of the Lord's meal, there comes an awareness of God in our midst. Some words of the traditional Roman Catholic mass point to a principle that defines the potential of our holiness as humans: "We share in the divinity of Christ, who has humbled himself to share our humanity." We don't become God, of course, but we are privileged by divine grace to be God-indwelt and thus increasingly God-like.

In the Eucharist (the thanksgiving feast of the Lord's Table), disciples are invited to confront in the loaf and cup a reality that confounds our ordinary speech and outruns our typical view of what is and could/should be. Ordinary bread, when viewed in relation to Jesus Christ, becomes holy. That's not just when we kneel to take a bite and remember the cross of Jesus. The ordinary bread we encounter on any table the next or any day should retain for us a lingering sense of Sunday's sacredness.

All bread is a gift from God's hand, given for our nourishment, but also to be received with gratitude and shared. So how one handles bread is a sign of true discipleship and Christian holiness.

Our culture encourages us to be sturdy individuals, self-sufficient folks, "real" men and women who are always eating (buying and selling) as much as possible. In bold contrast to this is the instruction of our Lord: "Then he looked up at his disciples and said: 'Blessed are you who are poor, for yours is the kingdom of God. Blessed are you who are hungry now, for you will be filled'" (Luke 6:20–21a). Mahatma Gandhi once said: "Live *simply* so that others might have a chance to simply live at all!" He was echoing Jesus.

The arrival of God's kingdom is pictured in the Bible as a big party, where tears are wiped away and "all peoples" are invited to come, dine, and rejoice. The Pharisees grumbled because Jesus was already sending out the invitations—to the wrong people. He ate with Zacchaeus, talked gently and forgivingly to a prostitute caught in the act, recruited as disciples men who were Zealots and tax collectors. It was just all wrong or, as Jesus proclaimed, amazingly all right! He was doing no less than "re-inventing the Kingdom of God *around his own work*; and at the heart of it was the great sign of welcome to all-comers, welcome to the party, to the Messianic Banquet, to the renewed people of God. Jesus was offering all and sundry the daily bread that spoke of the Kingdom of God."[6]

So when we pray for bread, our prayer should highlight what is implied in Matthew's version of the Lord's Prayer. The original Greek can be rendered, "give us *today* our bread for *tomorrow*." We declare ourselves ready to receive the first bites of that bread of heaven promised to be spread lavishly in God's great tomorrow. The disciples knew in part, and soon would know even more, about the coming of that amazing bread. They knew Jesus had fed thousands with a handful of food. They soon would experience the "Last Supper" where they would be handed a bit of bread and a sip of wine and told that they were the first tastes of eternal nourishment. They would soon be shocked to see the bloody crucifixion of Jesus and then the stunning resurrection, an event dramatizing God's promise that the divine kingdom is victor over even death. Certainly, God was capable of meeting all their essential needs in the meantime.

So our Lord directs us to pray in a way quite parallel with that glorious invitation found in Isaiah 55:1:

> Ho, everyone who thirsts,
> Come to the waters;
> And you that have no money,
> Come, buy and eat!
> Come, buy wine and milk
> Without money and without price.

6. Wright, *Lord and His Prayer*, 39–40.

A Materialistic Faith

Christianity is materialistic. This statement would be outrageous if it meant valuing material things above full devotion to God. Jesus, however, spoke of a different kind of materialism. He called people to enlist in God's kingdom, embody God's reign *in this world*, and thus learn to see things as simple and basic as bread through eyes that are spiritually aware. Personal holiness is not the unnatural elimination of needs and desires basic to being human. Rather, it is placing such needs and desires in the immediate path of God's judging and honoring, asking that what we wish be satisfied how, when, and why God chooses.

Physical people wanting physical bread is natural and appropriate, of course. Three things, however, often go wrong with our natural desires.

First, we may elevate our confidence in God's giving to the point that we become lazy. There is a "synergistic relationship between divine providence and our own labor."[7] Paul emphasizes the gracious giving of God but also insists that anyone too lazy to provide for his own household is worse than an unbeliever (1 Tim 5:8). Holiness involves serious effort to produce the fruits of honest labor.

Second, we may want much more than is necessary, and at the expense of others. If we crave more and more, as though a full belly will satisfy a hungry soul, we run the risk that the spiritual dimension of our lives will be washed away in the garbage of our many meals. Remember that the "our" which prefaces the Lord's Prayer has a particular significance here. The bread that God gives us is *family* bread. One hymn says well what Jesus intends to instill in us: "Breathe through the heats of our desires thy coolness and thy balm." The disciple should pray, not only for bread, but for balance and balm.

Third, we may give in to the temptation that Jesus resisted as from the devil—turning stones into bread. This is the temptation to get something for nothing. We want and want and hope to gain more and more for little effort, even for no effort, if possible. We buy lottery tickets as a way of becoming suddenly rich for no effort, except

7. Sproul, *Prayer of the Lord*, 67.

to risk a few dollars. We devalue and avoid hard work whenever possible. However, Jesus painted a very different picture. Spiritual balance places an appropriate value on material things, not denying their importance and necessity in this physical life, but asking for what is truly needed and extending compassion to any who have less than they need. Christianity does not share the tendency of Buddhism to disdain all human desire and to ignore all want. Rather, it affirms the goodness of creation; it recognizes the legitimacy of physical existence and its regular needs; it engages in honest work to obtain what is necessary; and it celebrates all that becomes available to us as a divine gift.

With all of the deep biblical meanings of the phrase "bread of life," there yet is the need for actual bread. The Greek word *epiousios* ("daily," as in Matthew's account of the Lord's Prayer) is rare indeed in Greek literature at the time of Jesus. Only recently was an extrabiblical papyrus found with this word on it. It was a woman's shopping list! We do have to go shopping periodically, and God invites us to give him our shopping lists. But, while shopping, we also are to be hallowing God's name and seeking to do his will. We can walk the aisles of the grocery store while trusting God's provision for each day's need—our own and those of others.

God cares for our *bodies*, not just our *souls*. So should we. In this important sense, Christianity has been called the most materialistic of all the world's religions. True followers of Jesus gladly feed the hungry, care for the orphans, build hospitals, and so on. David Elton Trueblood comments: "To say that what happens to our bodies is unimportant is simply not true. Therefore, our spiritual message is not likely to mean much to hungry people unless we first help them to be fed. The philosophy of Christ is the philosophy of *wholeness*."[8]

Despite the actions of some religious radicals, the path to mature spiritual life involves caring for our bodies, not starving and beating them as though the escape from our bodily existence would deliver us into God's presence. The temples of God, our bodies in which we live for now, are to be treated as sacred sites of divine residence. So are the needy bodies of others. So when we ask for "our" daily

8. Trueblood, *Lord's Prayers*, 53.

bread, we will exert every effort to make the prayer come true for us *and others*. Let's remember that Jesus did not teach us to pray to "give me my bread," but to "give us our bread." Prayer for oneself alone is sinful, because prayer without works of compassion is dead.

So we ask as needy humans and as disciples of Jesus who are called to tasks well beyond our own resources. We hear Jesus say, "Ask and it will be given to you; seek and you will find; knock and the door will be opened to you" (Matt 7:7). In this hearing, however, we must be aware that his reference was primarily to our seeking and then receiving the reign of God in our lives, the kingdom realized in us. That is what Jesus was emphasizing in his Sermon on the Mount, the context of the Lord's Prayer.

Although he invites us to present our material "shopping list" in prayer, the Lord is not committed to accommodating whatever shopping list we come up with. His promise is that in asking we will receive—if we ask it as a result of our thirst and hunger for God and the righteousness Jesus described and modeled. It is God's good pleasure to give us the kingdom, to equip us for living a Christlike life in this world.

Discussion Guide

1. Do you believe that practical things such as daily bread are really God's concern? Is it selfish of us to ask for such things from a holy God?
2. Some of the first disciples of Jesus were fishermen. Why might they call the Sea of Tiberias the "Sea of Jesus"?
3. It seems odd to claim that Christianity is a materialistic faith. In what sense is such a claim justified?
4. Explain what Dr. Callen means by the statement that the daily bread God gives is "family bread." Do you agree?
5. Do you agree with the Hebrew claim that we aren't bodies *and* souls, but body-souls? Is there any practical difference?

Do Unto Others

"How dare we beg for grace with no intention of extending that same grace to others. How impudent of us to plead for forgiveness while harboring bitterness and resentment against others."
—David Timms

CHAPTER 6

Forgive Us Our Sins

It may seem quite a leap, but it really isn't. The Lord's Prayer moves from asking God to provide daily bread, thus sustaining our lives in this world, to asking for the forgiveness of our sins, a necessary preparation for life in the next world. This move is quite natural in a biblical context because the Bible often makes a connection between food, sin, and forgiveness.

Sin is like eating (Prov 19:28 and 30:20). And as we all know, many people sin by how they eat or by how they restrict the eating potential of others. The first sin is gluttony and the other greed. Sin originally came into human experience when our first parents ate inappropriately. They took forbidden food and ate it in defiance of God (Gen 3). Jesus fed Peter breakfast before restoring him to fellowship (John 21). The Lord's Supper uses simple elements we normally consume to symbolize the great act of God in Christ to provide our salvation from sin. The forgiving father in the parable of the prodigal son threw a feast to celebrate the return of the wayward (Luke 15:11–31).

In the ancient Near East, eating together was a sign of peace and friendship and, if necessary, reconciliation. In our Lord's wonderful invitation (Rev 3:20), he promises that if we open the door to him, he will enter and eat with us! Food is a tangible necessity. Forgiveness, maybe less tangible, is no less necessary for our human well-being now and hereafter. In our lost and sinful condition, we are invited to "taste and see" that the Lord is truly good, and happy are we if we seek refuge in him (Ps 34:8).

Guilt for What Exactly?

This element of Jesus' prayer is a problem for many contemporary Christians. Our surroundings are always trying to tell us that we have no guilt requiring forgiveness. We see no clear distinction between right and wrong—it's all a matter of genetic predisposition, personal preference, and the standards of our particular community that are not to be critiqued by another. Instead of judging others for their attitudes and actions, we are told, we should be tolerant of whatever they think and do. Guilt implies responsibility for wrongdoing, but little is supposedly left today in the wrongdoing category. We're glad to eat, but slow to repent.

The Lord's Prayer covers the basics of our needy human lives and consciously counters the indulgent stance of today. It teaches, by contrast, that once we have properly oriented our lives to God, learned reverence, released our stubborn grip on our own selfish wills, asked that we be guided into the proper way of life under God's reign, and sought the bread we need to make the journey, still another great need remains. Guilt turns out to be very real for all of us. Our past follows and sometimes comes close to crippling us in the midst of our launching into new life with Christ. Living in humble reverence for a holy God tends to remove the self-justifying cover that numbs and blinds us from the deserved pain of actual guilt. We have all gone wrong and need divine forgiveness. Our prayer must address this reality.

Isaiah had barely finished hearing the seraphim say, "Holy, holy, holy is the Lord of hosts" (Isa 6:3) when he had to blurt out, "Woe is me! I am lost, for I am a man of unclean lips, and I live among a people of unclean lips; yet my eyes have seen the King, the Lord of hosts!" (v 5). No wonder Jesus includes in our Prayer a plea to the Father for forgiveness. That wasn't his personal need (John 8:46), but he knew it always would be the need of his disciples. We all have the weight of our yesterdays, though we now are determined to face new tomorrows with our Lord. This weight must be lifted by the graciousness of God.

The Old Testament, the Hebrew Bible of Jesus, is filled with the failures of Israel to live up to her high calling under God. We are haunted still by what God once said to his people through the prophet Hosea: "I will go back to my place until they admit their guilt. And they will seek my face; in their misery they will earnestly seek me" (5:15). Disciples of Jesus must come to understand their need for forgiveness and not neglect appealing to the Father for the resolution of their guilt. We'll never stand tall until first we bow low.

What Do We Owe God?

At this point, we should give careful attention to a particular word in the Lord's Prayer. *Debts* is the word used in Matthew 6:12, with *sins* in Luke 11:4. There is good reason to think that Matthew is closer to the actual Aramaic language of Jesus. If so, the natural first thought we have upon hearing *debts* should include economics. Unremitted debts were a common form of injustice in Old Testament times. The Old Testament is full of references to Sabbath creation, Sabbath day, Sabbath year, and even a Sabbath jubilee that was to include the resting of fields, the remitting of financial debts, and the actual freeing of debt slaves. This liberation theme was based on the Book of the Covenant, the oldest legal section of the Bible (Ex 20:22–23:33). There God boldly identifies himself as the one who brought the chosen people out of the land of Egypt, out of the house of slavery (v 2). Being the heirs of such gracious saving, how dare any Israelite ever permanently enslave another?

God stands for *distributive* justice and *restorative* righteousness—sharing fairly with others and graciously forgiving their debts. A careful review of the Old Testament background of this complex subject indicates that the phrase "forgive us our debts, as we also have forgiven our debtors" should be taken more than metaphorically. "What—literally—do we owe to God?...People are created *in God's image* as stewards of the world...We owe it to God to run God's world responsibly...We owe God collaboration in hallowing God's name, in establishing God's kingdom, and in doing God's will 'as in heaven, so also on earth.'...We owe it to God to ensure that there is enough food and not too much debt in God's well-run Household."[1]

We have long been taught that we need forgiveness with respect to our personal acts of defying God's will, so it is important to note this additional biblical emphasis: We are responsible for and have failed in matters of economic and political stewardship. Many Christians are uncomfortable when the preacher announces a sermon on money. So be it. Politics is an especially difficult arena to negotiate by faith. So be it. As we pray, we face the God who is righteous and just, and expects the same of us in all dimensions of life.

In all likelihood, someone owes us money, and too many of us carry a credit card or two with high numbers and a very high interest rate. We can't expect capitalistic secular societies to function by God's standards, so we seldom see debt forgiveness modeled before us.

Some of us may be fortunate enough to be debt-free in relation to others; even so, our moral account books are yet in the red in our relationship to God's demands and expectations. There are no exceptions. "If we say we have no sin, we deceive ourselves, and the truth is not in us" (1 John 1:8). We all are in debt in one way or another, and we cannot repay all the debt on our own.

Once we have good perspective on the word *debt* and admit that we all are carrying it (especially in relation to God), we come to another important issue. It is one of singularity versus plurality. The Lord's Prayer asks God to forgive us as we forgive others. The corporate "our" of the opening "our Father" is significant here as elsewhere in the prayer. We typically think of sin as a personal problem. It is indeed, but every one of us has also grown up in settings dominated by corporate and communal sins. We may not have started them and may not be solely responsible for them, but we are part of them. We are sometimes voluntarily, sometimes unconsciously the beneficiaries of unjust systems, but we are participants in them nonetheless.

A young man finds himself conscripted into the military with a gun placed into his hands, and without clarity about the morality of what he might be ordered to do. A large landowner in the southern

1. Crossan, *Greatest Prayer*, 154, 155.

United States in the 1850s could well have been a serious Christian and also a large slave-owner. A woman in the United States of the 1990s might have had a large investment in mutual funds, tithed to the church the earnings from her investments, and not have been aware that her money was being used by others for purposes she would strongly disapprove of were it her personal decision. The federal income tax bill for the year comes and we pay because we must as citizens (unless we choose jail). Yet we are aware that our tax money is spent on some purposes that we would never support personally.

The point is, we all are enmeshed in complex social systems that are not easily changed. These systems may have genuine good in them, but they also tend to institutionalize things that many Christians would consider wrong, with our money and implied support behind them. On the personal level, we must repent, seeking God's forgiveness and our actual transformation. On the broader corporate level where we also live, repentance and its results are harder to define or implement. We, at least, should keep this in mind: "In commanding us to forgive, Jesus is inviting us to take charge, to turn the world around, to throw a monkey wrench in the eternal wheel of retribution and vengeance...So every Sunday the church reminds us that we gather as those who have been forgiven, for that is the way we plan to produce heroic souls who are able to forgive."[2]

We are all guilty, but guilty of what? We all are in debt, but to whom and for what? The Spirit of God makes us aware of our personal sin, which can then be addressed by our humble admission of it and the resulting divine grace to forgive it. The waywardness of social networks in which we participate is a more difficult matter to address. At least two things are clear: We cannot honestly pray for forgiveness without realizing our need for it, and it is unjust to receive our own forgiveness without freely extending it to others. There is no way out of our human dilemma except forgiveness, God's and then ours.

2. Willimon and Hauerwas, *Lord, Teach Us*, 84.

The Meanings of "Sin"

The New Testament uses different words for sin, more than an adequate range of meaning to gather us all under sin's shadowy pall. Just as *evil* is *live* spelled backwards, sin is existing backwards, living destructively, proceeding against the grain of God's intention.

The most common New Testament Greek word for sin is *hamartia*, an archery term that announces that the shooter has missed the target. Can any of us rightly claim that we are all that we might have been and should have been, having done all the good things we might and should have done? No. *Parabasis* is another New Testament Greek word for sin. It means "stepping across," violating the line between right and wrong. It is similar to the term *anomia*, "lawlessless," which describes a person who knows what is proper and deliberately defies the law, chooses the forbidden, and flaunts common decency like the man in Rudyard Kipling's poem "Mandalay":

Ship me somewheres east of Suez,
Where the best is like the worst,
Where there aren't no Ten Commandments,
An' a man can raise a thirst.

Still another New Testament sin word is *opheilema*, which is translated "debt" in Matthew's version of the Lord's Prayer. We can't avoid Paul's sobering judgment about our moral bankruptcy: "But by your hard and impenitent heart you are storing up wrath for yourself on the day of wrath, when God's righteous judgment will be revealed" (Rom 2:5). It is doubtful whether our good deeds can build up a treasury of merit, although we often speak of a faithful disciple adding "jewels to her crown." But Scripture makes clear that we can build up a treasury of wrath. A sinner is someone who has failed to pay God what is justly due, and there will be a reckoning day.

We disciples of Jesus, even after turning our backs on deliberate lawlessness, and no longer consciously stepping over God's line of right living, continue to have a sin problem. Some of our moral arrows still fail to land in the target's center; we still are not perfectly fulfilling our duty to serve God or selflessly love others. Our eternal destiny will always remain dependent on the sheer grace of God. But can we have any hope of escaping the bondage of our sin, here and now?

John Wesley understood sin as a deliberate violation of God's known will. Given this definition, we have hope in this life of fully aligning our wills with God's will. We can have a realistic hope of being sanctified, here and now, through the Spirit's purifying of our intentions. Yes, there always will be a gap between our intentions and the perfect performance of them. With our human limitations, we cannot do everything God intends and do it all in an ideal manner. Some level of debt to God and to others always will exist. Therefore, Jesus instructs us always to pray with humility, asking for the grace of God's forgiveness and the relief of our moral debt. But, even in the midst of our perpetual need, Scripture promises that we can align our wills and intentions with those of God. Such an alignment, regardless of human weakness and error, is God's goal and provision for us. To be so aligned is to be Christlike, and to be holy.

The Disturbing Word *As*

The love and forgiveness of God are unconditional—we can't earn or ever deserve them because they are gifts of grace. But Jesus adds an apparent condition to his disciples' forgiveness by God. It is a disturbing little word, *as*. We are to pray, "Forgive us our debts as we also have forgiven our debtors." Paraphrases David Timms: "How dare we beg for grace with no intention of extending that same grace to others. How impudent of us to plead for forgiveness while harboring bitterness and resentment against others."[3] The forgiveness of God in Christ is not pre-conditional—that is, we are not expected to clear all our debts and right all our relationships before God will forgive us. However, our forgiveness of others is clearly post-conditional; we must forgive others in order for God's forgiveness to remain with us. The forgiven must become forgivers.

3. Timms, *Living the Lord's Prayer*, 151.

Not to extend to others the love and forgiveness we receive so freely is surely to abort our reconciled relationship with God through our own selfish inaction. Consider the words of Jesus as he was dying on the cross, words paraphrased by Brennan Manning: "I know every moment of sin, selfishness, dishonesty, and degraded love that has disfigured your life, and I do not judge you unworthy of compassion, forgiveness, and salvation. Now, *you be like that with others*. Judge no one."[4]

My first theology professor in seminary carried the teaching burden of uncomplicating and practicalizing Christian theology. He had seen too many theology professors "parade their erudition and appear to teach and write for other profs." At age eighty-five, Dr. Gene Newberry's call was still to a "pilgrimage theology," and his testimony was simply this: "I call myself a progressive evangelical. God is closer than ever. Christ is sweeter than ever. The Kingdom is more important than ever. I'm not going to be picky or judgy about anything else. Playing God has never been appealing. This is a relief to me—and I am thankful."[5]

Proper Christian humility involves being open, gracious, and forgiving in our stance toward others, rejoicing in the few very important matters and not being "picky or judgy" about all the rest. As gracious and thankful Christians, we are called to be witnesses, not lawyers or judges. We should pursue the truth of God for spiritual growth and discipleship purposes, not for showing off our sophistication and building power blocks around our truth claims.

William Barclay finds this forgiven-and-forgiving the most frightening petition in the Lord's Prayer. The literal meaning is something close to: "Forgive us our sins *in proportion* as we forgive those who have sinned against us." In fact, he says, "If we pray this petition with an unhealed breach, an unsettled quarrel in our lives, we are asking God *not* to forgive us."[6] Again, this does not mean that all debts (financial, moral, and otherwise) must be repaid before God will forgive; it means that receiving God's forgiveness must inspire

4. Manning, *Signature of Jesus*, 63, 64.

5. Newberry, *Boy from Lewis County*, 95, 148.

6. Barclay, *Lord's Prayer*, 43.

a deep resolve in us to forgive all debts we possibly can, otherwise the floor of our own forgiveness will collapse under the weight of our choice to do evil—that is, to live life *backwards* despite the grace freely given to us. To pray "Thy kingdom come" and not to manifest its coming in our own attitudes and actions makes a mockery of our praying mouths.

Very soon after the disciples were instructed in this way by Jesus, they were shown by example exactly what he meant. The full grace of the Father resided in the Son, and the Son had to face the biggest debt imaginable. The prayer of Jesus in the garden shows the great struggle that we disciples sometimes face on a lesser scale. It is the human will in tension with the divine will. Here, Jesus became our prayer pioneer: "Not what I want but what you [God] want" (Matt 26:39). Jesus paid the debt of us all, covered the guilt of the entire creation, and released the captives by giving his one life for all lives, as an innocent man dying willingly on a cross. That dreadful hillside scene was a picture of God's loving heart spread across all the screens of the world. It was "finished," said Jesus. For us, however, forgiveness had just begun.

There is a warning in the story Jesus told about the unmerciful servant (Matt 18:23f). A certain king had forgiven a large debt of one of his servants. How did this forgiven servant respond? Now free of debt, he went out and selfishly started squeezing some people who owed him relatively small amounts. The king's forgiveness had reached the man's bank account, but not his heart. Because the forgiven servant did not follow through, the cancellation of his own large debt was voided, with the king saying angrily, "You wicked slave! I forgave you all that debt because you pleaded with me. Should you not have had mercy on your fellow slave, as I had mercy on you?...So my heavenly Father will also do to every one of you if you do not forgive your brother or sister from your heart" (Matt 18:32–35). God links his generosity toward us with our generosity toward others. If we do not forgive, the reconciliation of God will be nullified.

As we pray the prayer of Jesus, we begin having "the same mind, having the same love" that he had (Phil 2:2). The Lord's Prayer is given "so that Jesus' followers can breathe in what he's doing and so, with that breath, come alive with his life…Once we start inhaling God's fresh air, there is a good chance that we will start to breathe it out, too. As we learn what it is like to be forgiven, we begin to discover that it is possible, and indeed joyful, to forgive others."[7]

Christian holiness, then, is characterized in part by joyful forgiving. We can live such a crucified life of forgiving others only because the One who commands us is also the One who pioneered this path of forgiveness and now empowers us to walk it with him. Christ desires that all of us might share this testimony from Paul: "It is no longer I who live, but it is Christ who lives in me. And the life I now live in the flesh I live by faith in the Son of God" (Gal 2:20). How blessed such disciples are!

Forgiving, Forgetting, Feasting

Read the Lord's Prayer closely. Notice that it does not say we have forgotten what we have forgiven. Popular wisdom is that we've not really forgiven until we've forgotten wrongs done to us, just as God our Father, who is the great forgetter (Jer 31:34). Paul says that love "keeps no record of wrongs" (1 Cor 13:5). So, is Christian discipleship to be a kind of graceful amnesia?

Not quite. For us humans, forgetting is hardly possible and probably not even desirable. Seeking to forget the wrongs of the past is dangerously close to denying they ever happened, which virtually assures that they will be repeated in the future. To not forgive others is a serious error that jeopardizes our own forgiveness by God. But failing to remember what we have forgiven is full of significant dangers as we pursue our spiritual journey.

What Paul had in mind was surely something like this: Do not keep a record of the wrongs you have forgiven so that you can find ways to "get even" over time. A good memory is essential to spiritual growth, but using our memories for punitive purposes is to fall from God's grace and back into our own state of being unforgiven by God. Without good memory, "we have little ability to break the destructive

7. Wright, *Lord and His Prayer*, 56, 63.

cycles in marriages, families, and churches. Accountability depends on memory. Forgetting does little to challenge the perpetrator or change the future...In our memory, guided by grace and lathered with the love of the Father, lies our strongest future."[8]

Our being forgiven and then forgiving others, even though we continue to remember the wrongs (for constructive reasons only), is an example and celebration of the ancient biblical concept of a "jubilee year" (Lev 25). Every fiftieth year—basically, once in a lifetime—there was to be a festival of redemption and renewal among God's people. Debts were to be dissolved, slaves freed, and people released to return to their original homes if they wished—complicated as that would be. It was a time of great grace and a startling starting over. The economic ground was to be leveled, wrongs righted, yesterdays forgiven, and new doors to tomorrow opened wide.

John Killinger tells of a Christian worship service where jubilee was needed.[9] Before the preacher began his sermon, a man stood and shared his heart with the congregation. There was much unresolved conflict among the people, he said, some of it so old that people couldn't even remember the original issue—they just knew how they felt and who was to blame. The man said it was a black cloud blocking God's work among them. The minister put his sermon away, quoted Matthew 5:23–24 about reconciling before bringing one's gift to the altar, and declared a time of extended silence and waiting. Within minutes, dozens of people had moved to the sides of others, talking quietly, crying openly, and hugging tightly. Their jubilee year had come. Someone afterwards called that service a "feast of love."

Jesus came to announce a jubilee for all humanity. When the reign of God arrived with him, it was a festival of unlimited forgiveness. Jesus told his disciples, in effect, "You are to be hosts at this festival, showing the way by showering on others the gracious forgiveness that has been so generously showered on you!"

8. Timms, *Living the Lord's Prayer*, 153, 155.

9. Killinger, *God Named Hallowed*, 53–54.

Discussion Guide

1. Are you guilty of anything that requires divine forgiveness? Have you or will you seek that forgiveness rather than denying its need?
2. How *sin* is defined is crucial for our understanding of forgiveness and our hope of holiness in this life. How would you define it?
3. What is so disturbing about the tiny word *as* in the Lord's Prayer? Does the quality of our relationship with God depend in part on the quality of our relationships with others?
4. Have you ever judged another Christian prematurely, based mostly on appearances or your own personal preferences? Have you admitted your wrong and sought that person's forgiveness?
5. What about our forgiving others and then trying to forget the wrong they have done? Do you agree with Dr. Callen that we cannot forget how others have wronged us? If so, how can we prevent those memories from poisoning our relationships with them?

Be Warned!

Paul warns us, "Let anyone who thinks that he stands take heed lest he fall." (1 Corinthians 10:12 ESV)

CHAPTER 7
Deliver Us from Evil

The request for daily bread deals with our regular bodily needs; the request for forgiveness of debts is concerned with the resolution of our past sins. Now comes the petition for protection and guidance as we proceed into the future, seeking to honor God and be active agents of the divine kingdom. Faithful disciples of Jesus serving in this broken and sinful world certainly need protection from evil.

Jesus made clear to his disciples that they were in a spiritual war. He put it simply: "In this world you will have trouble" (John 16:33). The apostle Paul stated it just as bluntly with this instruction: "Put on the whole armor of God, so that you may be able to stand against the wiles of the devil. For our struggle is not against enemies of blood and flesh, but against the rulers, against the authorities, against the cosmic powers of this present darkness, against the spiritual forces of evil in the heavenly places. Therefore, take up the whole armor of God, so that you may be able to withstand on that evil day, and having done everything, to stand firm" (Eph 6:11–13).

Our faith will be confronted by evil, and we must be prepared to withstand that danger. Therefore, the Lord's Prayer cries out for God's constant help. In return, Jesus promises the comfort and guidance of his Spirit (John 16:13–14; Acts 1:4–5).

Tested and Tempted

No Christian prayer is complete without a frank recognition of the evil in this world, both in us and around us. Our eyes may be closed when praying, but our heads should not be stuck in the sands of denial. Jesus raised our awareness of this fact by identifying the last of the six petitions in the model Prayer.

Danger and death lurked just ahead for Jesus himself. He also knew that his disciples were confused, anxious, and under threat. The life of faith is a little like walking in an unmarked minefield; disciples must seek *enablement* and *protection*, the first to handle testings by God, the second to handle temptations thrust upon us by the forces of evil. Yes, it is important to understand that two kinds of challenges lie before us—one from God, intended for our good, and one from the evil one, intended for our spiritual destruction.

This portion of the Lord's Prayer, as with all the others, is grounded in the life and ministry of Jesus himself. His earthly life began on a very dark and cold night in Bethlehem. The circumstances could hardly have been worse, with not even a decent room for Mary to use in giving birth. Soldiers were about to be dispatched to find and kill Jesus. He had a price on his head almost from the beginning. A paranoid tyrant just up the road heard of his arrival, and panicked. Word had reached Herod that this tender little bundle might be a royal pretender, a threat to his power, so he sent his goons to snatch the child from his mother's breast.

Christian hope can see through such deep darkness. We can see, as just before the coming dawn, the rising of the Morning Star of God. Herod couldn't allow that Star to rise in his day; he wanted no new royalty parading around in his kingdom! He dispatched butchers, but they missed the baby Jesus. The baby would manage to grow up before another squad of butchers caught him and nailed him high for all to see. Jesus came to his own people, and even they rejected him (John 1:5). He realized his awkward beginning and his coming cross, and now he wanted his disciples to understand that they were to face similar dangers.

Immediately after his baptism, Jesus found himself in a desert place, wrestling with temptation, both clarifying what God wanted him to be and do and bracing himself for the difficult task of ministry. It was not to be easy, and he knew that the ministries of his disciples would also be stalked by pain and temptation. They had to be warned and prepared. A faithful life of prayer would be essential.

Jesus told them about his own temptations as a way of warning and instruction. He must have been the one to tell them, since he would have been alone with the great tempter. And since telling this experience was a choice of Jesus, it must have been of exceptional importance in his eyes. Trouble was ahead for all of them, so Jesus offered to be their shepherd, guiding his beloved sheep even in the dark valleys where death can await. They were weak and immature in their faith, just as we are. They needed to know two essential things about such times of trial, and so do we.

First, we must know that sometimes God tests us in order to assess how far we have come and to build our understanding and strength. Second, an evil one also tests us, but for a completely different reason. The evil one tries to exploit the times of divine testing and divert us into paths of destruction. The evil one tempts believers in Christ in every possible way, even using people and events in church life as tools of his dirty work. So it would be with Ananais and Sapphira (Acts 5) and the troublemakers in the church in Corinth (1 Cor 1:4–17, 5:1–6:20). Wherever possible, evil infiltrates the church and works from the inside (Phil 3:17–21; 2 Tim 3:1–9; 2 Peter 2:1–22).

We who seek to follow Jesus must be open to the testing by God, even if it's not always pleasant. At the same time, we must be on guard and ask God to deliver us from the evil that seeks our downfall. None of us is exempt. Paul warns us, "Let anyone who thinks that he stands take heed lest he fall" (1 Cor 10:12 esv).

Suffering Servants

Since the Lord's Prayer is rooted deeply in the life experience of Jesus himself, the context of the Prayer is far from pretty. About the time that Jesus was born, a Roman legion reacted to a Jewish revolt and marched right through the Nazareth vicinity to destroy nearby Sepphoris, the capital city of Galilee. Jesus must have heard often during his boyhood in Nazareth about awful things that happened that fateful year when the Romans came. From that village talk, surely tinged with bitterness and rebellion, what would Jesus have concluded about God and Rome, subservience and rebellion, violence and nonviolence? His answers lie just behind the Lord's Prayer.

How do God's servants survive and serve best in a violent world? How do we react to a Dietrich Bonhoeffer who was a prayerful Christian pacifist and yet, in an extreme set of circumstances in Nazi Germany, joined a plot to assassinate Adolf Hitler? Are we not called to sacrifice ourselves and serve through whatever suffering may become necessary? Is there one answer, one way for all believers to think and act in all circumstances?

In one of my college Bible courses, I was required to memorize and reproduce on the final exam the full text of the fifty-third chapter of Isaiah. We students complained, but the professor was unrelenting, seeing in this chapter a summation of the Jewish hope and the Christian fulfillment. The sacrificial lamb, seen later as Jesus himself, "was despised and rejected by others; a man of suffering and acquainted with infirmity…he has borne our infirmities and carried our diseases; yet we accounted him stricken, struck down by God, and afflicted. But he was wounded for our transgressions…and by his bruises we are healed" (Isa 53).

That was precisely what ancient Israel was to have been, God's lowly and self-giving agent of reconciliation to the world. That is what Jesus became. He was the "suffering servant" who reflected the very heart of God. Albert Schweitzer once said that Jesus was called to throw himself on the wheel of world history so that, even while crushing him, it might be forced to start turning in the opposite direction.[1] That's exactly what he did on that old rugged cross.

The ongoing progress of God's redemptive plan through the faithfulness of the disciples of Jesus is highlighted in the Lord's Prayer. It also appears in an older and more obscure prayer recorded in 1 Chronicles 4. Jabez got his name because his mother "bore him in pain," and he has become widely noted today mostly because of Bruce Wilkinson's little book *The Prayer of Jabez*. Jabez called on God to bless him, to "enlarge my territory," to keep the divine

1. Schweitzer, *Quest of the Historical Jesus*, 370–71.

hand on him, and to keep him from evil "that I may not cause pain!" (1 Chron 4:9–10).

This ancient prayer catches up so much of the heart of Jesus. Christian discipleship involves sacrificial pain, although it certainly does not seek to cause more pain. It longs to have its territory of effective service enlarged, not for personal fame or gain, and in spite of all associated pain, so that God's kingdom will come more fully as the divine will is done on earth as it is in heaven. However, this means that faithful discipleship has physical needs and faces mortal dangers. Thus, we have these two aspects of the Lord's Prayer, one related to God's testing us so that we might achieve spiritual maturity, and the other related to our temptation to do evil so that we might be distracted from God's will, which ends in death.

The Double Request

Testing is a better word than *temptation* for translating the New Testament word *peirazein*. William Barclay explains that "to tempt people is not so much to seek to seduce them into sin as it is to test their strength and their loyalty and their ability for service."[2] In his prayer instruction, Jesus gives us counsel similar to what any dedicated teacher would provide. That is to say, tests are part of the curriculum, essential for our continued growth as students. The Father never tempts his children to do evil. However, God does test our faith. After all, "faith that can't be tested can't be trusted."[3] Our faith must proceed in a dangerous world, yet we have this promise of Jesus: "In this world you will have trouble, but take heart! I have overcome the world" (John 16:33).

The Bible records various times when God chose to test his children. A classic story is recorded in Genesis 22 where Abraham is asked to sacrifice his son Isaac. God tested the maturity of Abraham's faith by asking if he would be willing to give up what was most precious to him, should God require it. Abraham passed the test and became the "father of many nations." God had no intent of bringing harm to Abraham or his son; he intended to test the patriarch's

2. Barclay, *Lord's Prayer*, 46.

3. Wiersbe, *On Earth as It Is in Heaven*, 118.

faith to further enhance it and thus extend his own loving mission in the world.

The disciples of Jesus also encountered this painful lesson. Jesus himself was the Lamb of God, the Isaac replacement. Would Jesus, in his humanness, be willing to do the Father's will, whatever the personal cost, even if it took him to an ugly Roman cross? Like Abraham before him, Jesus also would pass the test. First, however, he determined to help his disciples learn to pray for such self-surrender in their own ministries, to further the greater cause of God's kingdom. Paul pleaded three times that God would remove a painful affliction, which he called his "thorn in the flesh." Instead of removing it, God converted Paul's pain into ministry power, transforming his human weakness into strength (2 Cor 12:1–10).The beloved Psalm 23 speaks of God guiding his dear children along the right paths for his name's sake (v 3). The Hebrew word for *paths* was often used to describe travel routes with deep ruts made by heavily loaded carts on wet ground—no easy or safe way to travel! Even so, we have a shepherd guide who shows us the way, protects us from wild animals, picks us up when we fall, pulls us out of ruts when we get stranded, and places oil on our wounds when we are hurt. In this world, a smooth path is seldom available for our faith journey with God. Our trek entails dangers, tests, lessons, wisdom, and slow-emerging maturity—things we gain only by going where the Lord sends us and undergoing the tests he has for us.

The Bible is rich in wonderful imagery that illustrates our faith walk. One of the best images is found in Deuteronomy 32, which says that God tests his young children like a mother eagle tests her young. Her intent is to enable the next generation to be all it was created to be—even when some pain and fear are involved. The eagle teaches her young to fly, and fly they must to grow, survive, and reproduce. She urges them from the nest, but they naturally resist leaving.

How does a loving mother handle the fear and resistance of her children? According to this biblical image, she finally forces them out of the nest, takes them into the air, and releases them to what they likely think is their fate—although, in fact, it is to their intended future. "She swoops underneath them and catches them upon her broad back. Then she tosses them off again, and continues to repeat this procedure until they finally begin to flutter their wings and gradually learn to hold themselves aloft."[4]

God's people must endure God's tests until they graduate to airborne adulthood. All who really believe in God's love will leave the immature nest willingly, release control over their lives, and trust their future to God. Holiness grows as we continue leaving, learning, releasing, and trusting.

Abraham left Haran and all that was familiar to him, in order to begin a journey he had never made before to a place he had not seen before—without a map or GPS, only the promised guidance of God. He set out "not because he can predict the role he is to play in the history of salvation, but simply because of his personal experience, the spiritual experience of God speaking to him. There is no program he can detail; no insight into history with which he can support his decision; no model through which he can obtain a psychological identity. Spiritual experience has become a summons. It is God who directs. And the future is God's."[5]

God tests our faith and checks our readiness to serve by sending us into the future, both his future and ours with him. In the process, God does not tempt us as the devil did Jesus in the wilderness. A tempter hopes that the tempted one will fall. That has never been the intent of God, the Father of Jesus. He "cannot be tempted by evil, nor does he tempt anyone" (James 1:13). Testing, however, is a different matter. When God administers a test to us, he hopes to stimulate our urge to fly. He is measuring and refining us, never with the intent that we "crash and burn"; but if and when we do, he is still there, building and restoring us.

We disciples are reluctant to be tested. We ask the Master Teacher not to do any more testing than is absolutely necessary. Jesus understands this very human response but still admonishes us to pray earnestly for whatever we need to deepen our trust in God and become more like Christ in this world. Our prayers are much

4. Zodhiates, *Lord's Prayer*, 336.

5. Manning, *Signature of Jesus*, 15.

like that of the father who desperately wanted Christ to heal his son: "I believe; help my unbelief!" (Mark 9:24). We pray, "Please don't lead us to any more tests than necessary; still, regardless of how it needs to be, may your will be done!"

Then there is the other half of this petition in the Lord's Prayer. We'll accept the necessary *testing* from God—which apparently we need, even though, in our frailty, we wish we could avoid. What we dare not face alone is the intrusion of evil into our lives of faith, the malicious tempting that does not come from God. Perhaps this part of the prayer of Jesus may be paraphrased like this:

> As much as possible, O God, please spare me from any but the most necessary spiritual tests. I leave that to your judgment and know that they are for my spiritual well-being, but in my humanness I still shrink from them. Above all, dearest Father, please save me from the attacks of the Evil One who intends my spiritual destruction!

In this sense, when we pray the Lord's Prayer, we are being very intentional about clothing ourselves in Christ and shedding the rags of sin. What is evil? Words like *holocaust*, *terrorism*, *molestation*, and *murder* come to mind. The first Jewish disciples of Jesus would readily have thought of the hated Roman occupation of their land. For them, however—and equally for us—the most lethal expressions of evil are likely rooted in our own hearts, "not in foreign ideologies, tyrannical regimes, or demonic forces in distant places, but within our own hearts…anger, lust, jealously, greed, pride, aggression, bitterness, indifference, to mention just a few."[6]

Evil is the woman who claims to be a follower Christ in polite company and makes a mockery of him in private. Evil is the man who wallows in pornography and then denounces sexual deviance the next time he is in the pulpit. Evil is seeing the throngs of orphans in Africa because of AIDS, knowing that one has financial resources that could save some from an early death, but choosing to look the other way. In the immediate context of Jesus, evil was stirring up

6. Timms, *Living the Lord's Prayer*, 170, 171.

insurrection against the Romans in order to obtain freedom with the blood of others. Jesus had judged such violence a temptation of the devil when he was offered power over all the kingdoms of this world. The exercise of raw power for our own ends is not the divine strategy. Jesus soon would tell Peter to put down his sword (Matt 26:52). God's work must be done in God's way, even if it costs followers of Christ everything in this world.

Jesus looked right into the eyes of his disciples and said in effect, "I will test you to ensure integrity and enable growth, but I cannot tolerate the presence of evil. Pray earnestly that you will be delivered from evil. Only then will the kingdom of my Father come and his will be done here in this sinful place. It starts with me, and it must continue with you!"

Jesus expects his disciples to respond with a simple, "Even when my humanness asks that I not be led into testing, I will submit humbly to all tests of loyalty, integrity, and obedience. But, with the help of God, I will not yield to the temptation to do evil!"

The disciples had begun a new life of faith made possible only by the grace of a loving God. That same God would stand by them, test and strengthen them. However, their enemy was prowling around each thought they would have and every action they would take. So they were simultaneously victorious and vulnerable. Grace received was no guarantee that grace would be retained or used to best effect.

Soon the apostle Paul would confess, "Wretched man that I am! Who will rescue me from this body of death?" (Rom 7:24). The wonderful answer for him, and for all disciples of Jesus, is simply this: "The sting of death is sin, and the power of sin is the law. But thanks be to God, who gives us the victory through our Lord Jesus Christ" (1 Cor 15:56). Knowing this wonderful truth, we are to pray to the God of our beginnings that we will persist in faith so that he also will be the God of our endings! The journey between the beginning and end of our discipleship is often difficult, but by divine grace it is fully possible!

We so easily lose sight of God in the midst of the fray. We are tried in the fire; we are attacked by the enemy of our souls. But in all of this, we cling to a wonderful truth: "Our God is a hidden God, but in Jesus his ways have become known to us. In Jesus we see the Father. God is still in heaven waiting for us to complete our journey. But Jesus risen, with the power of the Holy Spirit, is in our midst, lighting the way."[7]

To summarize, the Lord's Prayer alerts us to be constantly aware of (1) testings from God, designed to mature our faith and enhance our service, (2) temptations from the evil one, waiting around every corner in hope of disrupting our faith, and (3) the loving and powerful presence of God, ever available to guide us through the testings and save us from the temptings. Our journey of faith is potentially the highway of holiness since we are accompanied by the Holy Spirit of God who wishes our growth into the likeness of Christ.

Discussion Guide

1. Explain the important difference between being "tested" and being "tempted."
2. Isaac Watts penned these lines: "Since I must fight if I would reign,/Increase my courage, Lord!" What must a Christian fight against? How does prayer help us to prepare for this fight?
3. Watts continues: "I'll bear the toil, endure the pain,/ Supported by Thy Word," and Dr. Callen confirms that discipleship involves "sacrificial pain." What aspects of the Christian life are painful for you? How does prayer help you deal with this pain?
4. Recall a time when you yielded to the temptation to do wrong. What steps did you take to deal with the consequences and with your guilt? Was prayer a part of the process?
5. Now recall a time when you resisted the temptation to do something wrong. How did prayer help you to resist?

7. Gafney, *A Guide to the "Our Father" Today*, 21.

God's Triumph

All that was, is, or ever will be finally will end and be accountable to God. The Lord's Prayer is all about God and ends in that final note of divine victory over all things. Here is the Prayer in brief outline:

- The fatherhood of God
- The holiness of God
- The kingdom of God
- The will of God
- The provision of God
- The forgiveness of God
- The protection of God
- The final triumph of God

CHAPTER 8

The Power and the Glory

Correct praying and true worship begin and end with holiness, first by the initiative of a holy God and then by our recognition, honoring, and participation in God's holy kingdom already coming and forever assured. This is why the Lord's Prayer begins with "hallowed be your name" and ends with "for yours is the kingdom and the power and the glory forever!" We might say that praying the Prayer given to us by Jesus is a way of pledging our allegiance to the divine King and his full reign; it is a loyalty oath that throws all other allegiances out the window.

In one paragraph of Jesus' birth narrative (2:1–14), Luke moves from the great emperor in Rome ("a decree went out from Emperor Augustus") to the unlikely birth of a new "king" to rule the whole world. When looking at baby Jesus, however, it would have been quite a stretch for any reasonable person to have thought that a makeshift cradle in a nowhere place could inspire people to pray, "Thine is the kingdom, and the power, and the glory!" But it soon would.

It should not be a concern that the final phrases of the Lord's Prayer are not in the earliest manuscripts we have of the Gospels written by Matthew and Luke. While the Prayer's concluding doxology first appears in manuscripts dating from the fifth century, already by the second century the longer ending was being recommended for use by the *Didache*, a manual of Christian worship and practice.

The glorious conclusion has been in wide use ever since, especially in the liturgies of the Protestant churches in the Western world.

This doxology was added for good reason. Jesus would almost certainly have ended his prayer instruction with something more than the abrupt phrase, "deliver us from evil." Whether he did or not, his disciples surely felt they had to end with a glorious benediction. What was added is fully consistent with the Prayer as a whole and is a direct echoing of David's ancient prayer of adoration to God, a prayer that Jesus probably knew and fully affirmed (1 Chron 29:10–13). It ends with, "You rule over all. In your hand are power and might; and it is in your hand to make great and to give strength to all. And now, our God, we give thanks to you and praise your glorious name" (vv 12–13).

The Ongoing Clash of Kingdoms

His name is almost as imposing as his outstanding body of musical compositions. Wolfgang Amadeus Mozart once composed a requiem mass for a citizen of Vienna. Unfortunately, Mozart died before it was completed, but his student(s) could not bear for the piece never to be finished or sung. They knew the composer's intent, were familiar with his musical techniques, and studied his remaining notes. So they proceeded to complete the composition. When the *Requiem Mass* in D minor is sung yet today, it rightly carries the name of Mozart, not those of his students.

And so it seems to have been with the prayer of Jesus for his disciples. As soon as they knew of the cross and resurrection and heavenly ascension of the Master, their hearts and prayers leaped with bursts of praise for the Bringer of life and the Conqueror of death. God's kingdom, after all, surely is the true and everlasting kingdom. His, and his alone, are the power and the glory, forever and forever! The final words of the Prayer may or may not have come directly from the mouth of Jesus, but they certainly are in full accord with his heart. The reality of the Prayer's benediction was and is our Lord's.

The bumper sticker on a car read: "There is only one God—so quit applying for his position!" But there always is a flood of divine applications. In this sin-drenched world, two kingdoms are destined to compete. The disciples of Jesus knew this, and also knew that help was on the way. Prophets had been foretelling it for centuries without knowing precisely who, where, or how deliverance would come. It was inevitable, however. The fallen kingdoms of this world are fragile and have no long-term future. The prophets knew that only the kingdom of God is forever. They knew the kingdom's coming was sure, and surely soon!

Augustus was sitting on the human throne in Rome. As had others before him, he had his foot on the throat of God's people. What he had no way of knowing, however, was that the time finally had come. The aging king in Rome was turning sixty when Jesus was born some fifteen hundred miles away. But more than the eastern Mediterranean Sea separated them. Their two kingdoms, so very different, were destined to clash. A few years later, Jesus tried to explain this to his disciples as he taught them to pray.

If Augustus had known about the Hebrew prophecies and now the little Jesus in a cowshed somewhere near Jerusalem, he likely would have reacted as Herod did. He would have tried to do away with this dangerous baby before he grew up and caused real trouble. Their two kingdoms were destined to clash. Why? Because they offered two radically different definitions of what true power and peace are all about. Augustus understood the effectiveness of his legions, feared worldwide, and was willing to accept the fact that many of his subjects regarded him as divine even before his death. He believed he must show no weakness or they would quickly change their minds.

Jesus would be regarded by his disciples, especially after his death and resurrection, as none other than God in human flesh, launching the divine kingdom of love and peace. The contrast with the powers and kingdoms of this world couldn't have been sharper, for those first disciples of Jesus or for us so many generations later. Jesus intentionally inaugurated his kingdom with a massive public show of weakness, a horrible death on a Roman cross. Somehow, in that weakness resided the power of God!

We continue to be faced with a double vision of reality each time we dare to pray as Jesus taught us. Who was right, the feared emperor of Rome or the angels who announced the Bethlehem birth and shocked the shepherds with, "Glory to God in the highest heaven, and on earth peace among those whom he favors" (Luke 2:14)? If we are willing to ignore the threats of the fearsome legions of worldly power and side with the fantastic declaration of the angels, then how easy, how natural, how wonderful it is to recognize that all parts of the Lord's Prayer are true and possible.

But how can this be? The Lord's Prayer claims so much about God and offers so much to the humble believer. It is true because, and only because, "Thine is the Kingdom, and the power, and the glory, forever and ever!" And since it is true and possible, those who pray this way are asking that this glorious and very different reign of God be fully realized in and through themselves.

The Prayer taught by Jesus encapsulates the whole life and work of Jesus. John sums it up in the beginning of his Gospel: "And the Word became flesh and lived among us, and we have seen his glory, the glory as of a father's only son, full of grace and truth" (John 1:14). Note that the glory spoken of in regard to Jesus was so different than that which supposedly surrounds the rulers of this world. When you look at the Word become flesh, "you don't see the sort of glory that Augustus Caesar and his like work for. You see the glory that is the family likeness of God himself. Caesar's glory is full of brute force and deep ambiguity. God's glory—Jesus' glory—is full of grace and truth. The royal babe in the cowshed overturns all that human empire stands for."[1]

We who now dare to speak to our Father God in intimate and expectant terms know ourselves to be anointed with the Spirit of Jesus to be the people of the real King over this old world. The inglorious glory of the poor little baby, highlighted in the powerless power of the cross, is nothing less than the strength of God that rules this world and the ages to come.

1. Wright, *Lord and His Prayer*, 82.

Defiant Cry of Faith

Imagine a large crowd seated long ago on a grassy hillside somewhere along the northern shore of the Sea of Galilee. They have been listening intently to an amazing teacher, a miracle worker, a gentle man speaking of the power of love and highlighting the virtues of humility. They are mostly the have-nots who languished under the power of military occupation. Rome and empires before it had brought to their little land amphitheaters, hippodromes, shining shrines to strange gods, magnificent palaces for the outside rulers, elaborate fountains, everything to serve the pleasure of the powerful. What could these lowly people on the hillside make of words that Jesus addressed to the Father and meant for their encouragement? It's not easy in such circumstances to believe that God has "all the power and glory, for ever and ever." If God ever would be in charge of all things, apparently he wasn't yet!

It's so easy to think of religious ideas as only pleasant theories when they are considered in the face of the Roman power (Gk., *dunamis*) and glory (Gk., *doxa*) that were all too real. The Greek word *dunamis* is the base of the English word *dynamite*. The Romans gloried in victory and control, and were more than capable of destroying anything or anyone in their way. So, unleashing a *doxology* (a praise prayer championing the glory of God) right in the face of the Romans would have seemed a bit ludicrous. No matter. That is exactly what Jesus said that his disciples are to do in their praying.

These words of doxology, classically a part of the Lord's Prayer, sound both seditious and pie-in-the-sky, a defiant claiming of allegiance to a new kingdom, but admittedly one that is invisible, with power that might be only the stuff of empty faith and hopeful delusion. On the other hand, kingdoms like Rome have come and gone over the centuries. Power based on swords, guns, and bombs corrupts those who wield it. They are destined for eventual death, felled in the end by the weapon of another.

Jesus was not calling for a grasping of swords, not for another empire to join the line of failed others, nor for the crowd on the hillside to become the politicians in Jerusalem or guerilla fighters in the back alleys of numerous towns. He was urging a confidence in the supremacy, sovereignty, and endurance of God's kingdom over all human institutions, philosophies, governments, and empires. Such confidence, if truly held, makes secondary all personal ambitions and group nationalisms. It finally settles the citizenship question. We are to give Caesar only what belongs to him (Matt 22:21), which isn't all that much!

We noted in a previous chapter that the Christian doctrine of Trinity (God as Father-Son-Spirit) had not been developed in Jesus' time. The trilogy of divine affirmations known well by Jesus and his hearers, the one echoed in the concluding crescendo of the Lord's Prayer, is Psalms 22, 23, and 24. This triune heartbeat of traditional Jewish faith lay deeply in the heart of Jesus. He would soon use words from Psalm 22 when dying on a Roman cross: "My God, my God, why have you forsaken me?" (v 1). The quieting answer would come from Psalm 23: "Even though I walk through the valley of the shadow of death, I will fear no evil, for you are with me." Then Psalm 24 bursts forth to sweep death and destruction off the stage of history: "Lift up your heads, O gates; and be lifted up, O ancient doors, that the King of glory may come in. Who is the King of glory? The Lord, strong and mighty… he is the King of glory!" (vv 7–10). Why can we pray with confidence "deliver us from evil"? Because God's "is the kingdom, the power, and the glory, forever!"

We disciples of today must hear this well because much in us resists hearing it. The kingdom in view is not ours, but God's. It is all too common to seek our share of fame, wealth, power, at least over our own lives. But Jesus' words of caution to his first disciples should be heard by us also. "Only as we relinquish our own pursuit of power and glory can we know the freedom of the kingdom and the richest blessings of the Lord's Prayer…It's counter-intuitive, but it's the kingdom way…Our hearts find healing when we lay down our passion for power and give up our grasp for glory."[2] Life is not all about our comfort and advancement; it's not about how God might manage to fit into our little lives. It's about how we have the amazing opportunity to fit into God's life with us.

2. Timms, *Living the Lord's Prayer*, 191, 192.

In this world, personal holiness does not consist so much in fixing all that is wrong with us. Nor is it about getting answers to all of our human questions, questions like How can I find the secret to get along better? Be less anxious? Less poor? Less out of control? Less pushed around by others and my circumstances? A holy life is not all about me, not in the first instance at least. Holiness is about truly belonging to Jesus Christ. To be holy is to hear the great multitude shouting, "Hallelujah! For the Lord our God the Almighty reigns... On his robe and on his thigh he has a name inscribed, King of kings and Lord of lords" (Rev 19:6, 16). Hearing this with our own ears and hearts, being changed by our joyous focus on that glorious truth, is the path to true holiness.

The Lord's Prayer insists that we will move forward in our walk with God only when we embrace surrender and engage in praise and humble service. When the apostle Paul testified that "I die every day!" (1 Cor 15:31), he wasn't parading his sacrificial religiosity like an arrogant Pharisee. He was merely affirming what Jesus taught his disciples: "Unless a grain of wheat falls into the earth and dies, it remains just a single grain; but if it dies, it bears much fruit" (John 12:24). The death of personal surrender to the Lord is our opening the door to true life, the holy life.

It is important to recall that holiness is not intended to be a private affair. The reconciling thrust of Christian holiness faces outward to a lost world. In addition, it is corporate in nature—that is, the whole church is to be the holy body of Christ in the world. Insisted the apostle Paul, Christ came "so that through the church the wisdom of God in its rich variety might now be made known to the rulers and authorities in the heavenly places. This was in accordance with the eternal purpose that he has carried out in Christ Jesus our Lord" (Eph 3:10–11). And how is this to occur? Returning to the doctrine of the Trinity, it is to be accomplished through the Holy Spirit, who is the Spirit of Jesus, who is the Son of God.

We are to pray with great thankfulness because of a wonderful truth. "Yours is the kingdom and the power!" These words refer to our present acknowledging of the presence of the Holy Spirit who provides the *dunamis* ("dynamite") of God that transforms life and makes Christian ministry possible. The Spirit shares with the church the enabling energy of God, exactly as Jesus said at the time of his ascension: "Stay here in the city until you have been clothed with power from on high" (Luke 24:49).

So, we have our mission command and power promise: "You will receive power when the Holy Spirit has come upon you; and you will be my witnesses in Jerusalem, in all Judea and Samaria, and to the ends of the earth" (Acts 1:8). Even so, "Many Christians today seem to be afraid of the Holy Spirit. There are denominations whose doctrine of the Trinity could be summed up, 'God the Father, God the Son, and God the Holy Bible.' They have the Bible but not the Spirit's power. They are sound in many ways but are so cold, formal and seemingly lifeless."[3]

By sharp contrast, here is how it should be: "Whatever happens, we are Christ's church, against which the gates of hell will not prevail. Particular churches may falter and languish, but the church universal will continue. We are not abandoned amid earthly struggles but enjoy the grace of perseverance *through the Spirit.*"[4] Here is a model holiness prayer, one that comes naturally when praying the Lord's Prayer with all one's mind and heart:

> Living flame of love, ever burn on the altar of my heart. Welcome, Holy Spirit! Come and renew creation. Breathe on these dead bones, fill us with hope, lead us into God's embrace…We adore you, Lord and giver of life; come to us and set us free. Be no more a stranger or a lost relation, but fill us up with your love.[5]

Ending Well

As I age, I watch others who are nearing the end of their lives and journeys of faith. A common hope they have is that they will end well, that the final stage of the journey will not spoil all that has gone before. I watched my first wife live her last months in our home, her

3. Kendall, *Lord's Prayer*, 180.
4. Pinnock, *Flame of Love*, 222.
5. Ibid., 247.

body slowly yielding to cancer, but her faith unrelenting. She showed a simplicity of trust, a concern for others, and an inspiring hope in Christ. She wanted her witness to be undamaged by the way she accepted death. She inspires me and all of us to follow the advice of the writer to the Hebrews: "Therefore, since we are surrounded by so great a cloud of witnesses [now including Arlene], let us also lay aside every weight and the sin that clings so closely, and let us run with perseverance the race that is set before us, looking to Jesus the pioneer and perfecter of our faith" (Heb 12:1–2).

We learn in 1 Chronicles how King David ended well the process of the people's great gathering of their offerings to God:

> Then David blessed the Lord in the presence of all the assembly; David said: "Blessed are you, O Lord, the God of our ancestor Israel, forever and ever. Yours, O Lord, are the greatness, the power, the glory, the victory, and the majesty; for all that is in the heavens and on the earth is yours; yours is the kingdom, O Lord, and you are exalted as head above all. Riches and honor come from you, and you rule over all. In your hand are power and might; and it is in your hand to make great and to give strength to all. And now, our God, we give thanks to you and praise your glorious name." (1 Chron 29:10–13)

David treated the most important thing as the most important. He acknowledged that God is holy (that is, prior to, sovereign over, and distinct from all other things) and the only hope that is or ever will be. Just as Jesus later would, David knew that the right place to begin is with a hallowing of God's name, a grateful acknowledgment of the holy Father who is in heaven. Here is another prayer that puts into words this right beginning:

> Father, above all else that is happening in my life,
> Help me to see you.
> Shift my focus from demanding my own agenda to
> worshipping you.

Teach me to be more fully present to your Presence.
May waiting and worshipping form the bedrock of my life.
Amen![6]

God's holiness brackets all of our experience of creation; it came before and will be ever after our time on this earth. This holiness is the being and character of God, and we disciples of Jesus must be intensely aware of, honoring of, and open to receiving and modeling this holiness. Only then can we have Christ in us and thus be in this world as Christ intends. Only then are we prepared to be empowered through his Spirit. Beginning with an appreciative awareness of the holy God, we who believe are called to come into a sharing of the divine holiness, and thus have hope of living and dying well.

There are the several petitions of the Lord's Prayer, the things for which we properly ask. We ask for God's name to be reverenced. We ask for God's reign to truly come and his will to be really done, here and now. We ask for bread to sustain life, forgiveness for the past, and the will to forgive others. We ask for the grace to endure necessary testing, and that a divine shield be placed around us against the invasion of evil. Having adored, having surrendered, and having asked, there is always a choice to be made. We can "either love because we hope for something *from Him*, or we can hope *in Him* knowing that he loves us."[7] There is an important difference between these two hopes. Spiritual maturity is moving from the former to the latter.

We end the Lord's Prayer, then, by confessing with joy our awareness of God's unlimited power and glory. Even more, we end with an overwhelming awareness of God's love that focuses that power and defines and even shares that glory with us. Rather than demanding anything from God as a result of our prayer, we kneel in humble joy, we bask in the warmth of divine love, and we find our lives becoming more loving expressions of God's life and mission. Our being and doing as Christian disciples become genuine acts of worship. As we wait on God, praying as Jesus teaches us, "We release

6. Timms, *Sacred Waiting*, 65.

7. Merton, *No Man Is an Island*, 16.

all else and thereby enable the Lord to give us all things, which we receive authentically, not in *ownership* but as *stewardship*."[8]

As receivers and then sharers of divine love, as believers now tasting the holiness of the divine, we should never doubt the power of God to deliver us from the evil that seeks our downfall. Yes, the Father God whose name we hallow and whose kingdom we hope will soon come can "keep you from falling"! (Jude 24). Nothing surpasses the doxology that Paul shared with the Roman church: "O the depth of the riches and wisdom and knowledge of God! How unsearchable are his judgments and how inscrutable his ways!... For from him and through him and to him are all things. To him be the glory forever. Amen!" (Rom 11:33, 36).

Discussion Guide

1. Should we be troubled that the concluding benediction of the Lord's Prayer, as typically known and used by Protestants, is not found in the Bible? Why or why not?
2. The contrasting kingdoms of Augustus and Jesus both dealt with weakness. How were they so different if weakness was there for both?
3. There's a paragraph in the middle of this chapter that begins with, "In this world, personal holiness does not consist so much in fixing all that is wrong with us. What does it say holiness is and is not?
4. Dr. Callen says that we become more spiritually mature as we move from hoping for things *from* Christ to hoping for things *in* Christ. What do you believe he means?
5. The Lord's Prayer is bracketed by a necessary right beginning and a glorious right ending. What are they? Do your prayers follow this model pattern?

8. Timms, *Sacred Waiting*, 73.

The Biblical Mandate

So roll up your sleeves, put your mind in gear, be totally ready to receive the gift that's coming when Jesus arrives. Don't lazily slip back into those old grooves of evil, doing just what you feel like doing. You didn't know any better then; you do now. As obedient children, let yourselves be pulled into a way of life shaped by God's life, a life energetic and blazing with holiness.

—1 Peter 1:13–16 MSG

CHAPTER 9

Living a Holy "Yes!"

New Testament writers often conclude prayers with an *amen*. Like the *shalom* of the Hebrew Bible, this word has a core meaning and a series of surrounding and nuanced meanings. Rather than translating such words into one flat and inadequate English word, our Bible translators usually let the word stand in the original language, like the words *hosanna* or *hallelujah*. We can be confident that when biblical people ended a serious conversation with God by saying "Amen," they meant a lot more than, "That's done. Time to move on to something else."

One can easily sense the added burst of meaning conveyed in the original ending of Paul's second letter to Timothy: "The Lord will rescue me from every evil attack and save me for his heavenly kingdom. To him be the glory forever and ever. *Amen*!" (2 Tim 4:18). You can feel the "Wonderful!" and the "Yes!" in this "Amen!"

Many biblical prayers end with flourishes of joy and thanksgiving. They are marked dramatically with the exclamation mark of *amen*! The meaning of *amen* is a verbalized outburst of the soul of the person praying, an assurance that expresses acknowledgment, wonder, agreement, commitment, and sturdy confidence. If one English word had to suffice, it probably would be *Yes!* God's wonderful *yes* to us in Jesus Christ is to be reciprocated by our giving a big *yes* back to God. We find ourselves reaching out affirmatively to the One who has reached out so affirmatively to us.

The *amen* that ends the Lord's Prayer is really the keynote for our beginning. Having laid out our lives before God in the phrases of the Prayer itself, we end with the great word of faith and commitment, *Amen—Yes*. We realize that we have prayed our way into God's will and manner of being and living. Now it's launch time for existence in the Spirit of Christ! We have been called to begin new life, a life of faith, not cheap belief that somehow all of our life circumstances will turn out just fine. God did not promise to manipulate everything for our good pleasure. Rather, we place our faith in the One who sits above time and is in charge of eternity. The writer to the Hebrews asks that the God of peace will "make you complete in everything good so that you may do his will, working among us that which is pleasing in his sight, through Jesus Christ, to whom be the glory forever and ever. *Amen!*" (Heb 13:20–21, emphasis added).

Perfect Commitment to Christ

When completing the Lord's Prayer with a sincere *amen* put forth in honest faith, we have begun the disciple's path to perfection, certainly not of our life performance, but of complete commitment to the One through whom we now live and to whom belongs the glory, for ever and ever, Amen! This "Yes!" is the settled place deep within us where the healing and enabling waters of Jesus Christ run quiet and deep and always. We have prayed the prayer of Jesus who, according to John of the Apocalypse, himself carries the title *amen*: "These are the words of *the Amen*, the faithful and true witness, the ruler of God's creation" (Rev. 3:14, emphasis added). We can call Jesus the complete "Yes" because he was faithful unto death, the true witness to the identity and purpose of God the Father, and the ultimate ruler of all that is.

Christianity should be the pursuit of experienced and lived holiness in Jesus Christ, enabled by the Spirit. It should be the fellowship of the "saints" gathered for learning and service as the church, the body of Christ. It is "not a moral code to live by but a Person to live with and for; not a philosophical system or a collection of positive ideas but a Lord who embodies it all."[1]

Paul told the Corinthians that "all the promises of God in Him [Jesus] are *Yes*, and in Him *Amen*, to the glory of God *through us*" (2 Cor 1:20, emphasis added). God's angel told the compromising Laodicean church that Jesus is the *Amen* in contrast to themselves. The commitments of that congregation were mixed—drifting from a clear *yes* in Christ to a mushy *maybe,* caught in the morass of themselves. Holiness dares to look away from all the *maybes* and throw itself into the cleansing pool of God's redeeming grace where the fullness of the *Yes* resides.

A woman once said this about the holiness evangelist E. Stanley Jones: "Apart from the Holy Spirit, Brother Stanley would be a mess." Jones reports her comment in his wonderful autobiography, freely admitting that she was right. He adds this, however: "But with the Holy Spirit I am not a *mess*, but a *message*."[2] What a difference!

We should watch our discipleship language. Disciples deeply committed to Christlike being and living sometimes betray with their language an excessive preoccupation with the pursuit of behavioral *perfection*. They think that they know what that is in numerous particulars, the dos and don'ts that are to control the details of life and be pushed on others as mandatory standards. They speak repeatedly with words of obligation, duty, and demand, such as, "I ought," "I must," "I dare not," "and the same goes for you!" They so want to be pleasing to God, to appear completely separated unto God (be "holy"), to avoid even the appearance of any evil, and to be clearly different than the sinfulness around them. Often they take themselves and their moral judgments too absolutely. They won't tolerate the fact that they are still fallible human beings—which we all are. They edge toward hypocrisy, even from the best of motives, and lose their sense of humor, especially the ability to laugh at themselves and be patient with others.

Many Christians are not fun to be around. They are careful not to be seen with "sinners" and in places that may not be considered

1. Timms, *Living the Lord's Prayer*, 214.

2. E. Stanley Jones, *Song of Ascents*, 26.

holy. They have virtually abandoned the relaxed freedom of grace and are trying to please God in the realm of law observance, whose particulars were set by the standards of the fellowship of believers they choose to be with (although they are sure it all comes directly from God). This is not a new problem. The first generations of Christians, many of whom had been Jews, labored to determine the proper relationship of the free grace of God in Christ and the highly defined system of religious behaviors they had known and honored as traditional Jews.

The law-freedom struggle fills the pages of the New Testament. Paul heralded a new freedom in Christ and was criticized sharply by some as a worldly and dangerous libertine. He understood the gospel of Christ to be marked by freedom, gratitude, joy, a life of "I want to do this because of Christ!" rather than "I will do this because I must." Christians are to pray and live as resurrection people, rising from the waters of baptism with an infectious testimony of fresh joy and really good news for all people. That joy is to foster a culture of grace, the church, in which others are encouraged to come and also find new, real, and highly attractive life.

The great "Yes!" so needed in the church today is a hearty acceptance of the call of God for the holiness of his people. The heart-cry of Jesus for his first disciples has not changed with the passing of time. He prayed so earnestly to his Father on behalf of his disciples. In John 17 we see clearly what Jesus assumed would be the result of his disciples' praying his model Prayer with all their hearts and then lives: self-surrender before a holy God. This surrender to the gracious liberty in Jesus would yield a holy people who are delivered from evil and ushered into a redemptive community of faith that we call the church. According to Jesus, the church should be a unified Christian community, together in Christ on behalf of a lost world not yet ready to pray with the Lord. The Lord's Prayer is something of a "holiness manifesto" delivered by Jesus to his disciples, for then and for now. It is a call to center on what is most important.

John Wesley spoke of three main doctrines—repentance, faith, and holiness—which he once pictured as the porch, door, and interior of the house of real religion. The heart of the religious quest is only inside the house. Only there does one encounter the full potential of divine love, the experience of holiness, joyous service, and enduring hope. However, Wesley saw many professing Christians pause on the porch, maybe even approaching the door of this house, but without swinging it open and going inside. The question he posed to his ministers, then, was: "Are you going on to perfection?"

The goal of Christian faith involves the "fruit of the Spirit," divine life traits like those identified in Galatians 5:22–24. When our character and behavior can be traced back to the presence and functioning of this fruit of Christ's Spirit, then we have arrived by divine grace to what Wesley calls "sanctification" or "perfect love." We are inside the house of real religion. There may be much yet to explore and experience there, but at least we are actually inside!

Early lines from a hymn of John's brother, Charles Wesley, express the heart-cry of every earnest believer who has listened carefully to Jesus and now is praying in his special way. It involves the decision to say "Yes!" to God and do all that God expects and offers. It means exercising faith in a holy God who calls us to enter boldly through the door into the heart of religion, into holiness and perfect love—not arrogantly (for it's always by God's grace), but with repentance and humility and rejoicing.

Love divine, all loves excelling,
Joy of heaven to earth come down,
Fix in us Thy humble dwelling,
All Thy faithful mercies crown.
Jesus, Thou art all compassion,
Pure, unbounded love Thou art;
Visit us with Thy salvation,
Enter every trembling heart.[3]

We now have exhausted and maybe been exhausted by one decade of the twenty-first century. Frightening words such as *terrorism* and *recession* have dominated the headlines. Unfortunately,

3. Charles Wesley, "Love Divine, All Loves Excelling," *Worship the Lord: Hymnal of the Church of God* (Anderson, IN: Warner Press, 1989), 252.

the church that carries the Christ tradition today is too much like those first disciples of Jesus—still immature, anxious, confused, and divided from each other, still standing around on the porch of the holiness house. The first-century need is still ours today. According to the "Holiness Manifesto" released by concerned Christian leaders in 2006,

> there has never been a time in greater need of a compelling articulation of the message of holiness. People in churches are tired of our petty lines of demarcation that artificially create compartments, denominations, and divisions. They are tired of building institutions...They want to know the unifying power of God that transforms. They want to see the awesomeness of God's holiness that compels us to oneness in which there is a testimony of power...God is holy and calls us to be a holy people [4]

A modern translation of the Lord's Prayer in Eugene Peterson's paraphrase of the Bible, *The Message*, conveys in fresh words the prayer of disciples, the one that Jesus would have us pray.

> Our Father in heaven,
> Reveal who you are.
> Set the world aright;
> Do what's best—
>   as above, so below.
> Keep us alive with three square meals.
> Keep us forgiven with you and forgiving others.
> Keep us safe from ourselves and the Devil.
> You're in charge!
> You can do anything you want!
> You're ablaze in beauty!
>   Yes! Yes! Yes!

4. See Appendix A for the complete text of the manifesto.

By praying the Lord's Prayer often, our awareness of the presence, provision, providence, and power of God grows. As it does, we are encouraged more and more to exclaim with our hearts, words, and lives, "Yes!" This affirmation is a big step we need to take on our journey of faith.

We disciples of the Christ are to seek the point of faith, the milestone on the highway of holiness, that E. Stanley Jones finally reached in his own life. Here is his spiritually rich testimony, one about which Jesus surely would have smiled:

> So I live in a state of "Yesness," Yes to him [the Lord Jesus], primarily and absolutely; Yes to life and its responsibilities; Yes to approaching death; and Yes to the future, through and beyond death; Yes to his everything![5]

No one has summarized the essential elements of the Christian holy life better than Howard A. Snyder. Responding to the call of God by praying the Jesus way, with our words and our lives, we are enabled by the Spirit of God to become reflections of what God essentially is—*holy*. We can...

- Be filled with all the fullness of God in Christ, living holy, devout, pure, healing lives, being Jesus' counterculture and contrast society in witness to the world;
- Exercise a beautiful and effective array of ministries and callings, according to the diversity of the gifts of the Spirit;
- Be God's Kingdom people in the world, living in full allegiance to Jesus and his reign—Spirit-endowed coworkers for the kingdom of God;
- Live as a faithful covenant people, building accountable community, growing up into Jesus Christ, embodying the spirit of God's law in holy love;

5. E. Stanley Jones, *Song of Ascents*, 316.

- Care for the garden, this good earth, God's gift in trust to us, working in faith, hope and confidence for the healing of all creation, being the leading edge among the nations for the care and feeding and eventual reconciliation of all things—things visible and invisible; things in heaven and on earth. (See Ephesians 1:10, 22; 3:9; Colossians 1:16–20; Hebrews 1:2–3)[6]

The holiness of God's people rests in our decision to take the "yes stance" in our lives of faith. We say "yes" to the fullness of God in our lives, "yes" to the best possible use of God's ministry gifts we have received, "yes" to the fellowship and enrichment of other believers, "yes" to lives that nurture the well being of God's creation, and "yes" to the hope that one day the full will of God will be accomplished here and hereafter. Therefore, "the church which is filled with the Spirit and immersed in the compassionate care of a lost and afflicted humanity has one common longing, one unifying cry, one joyful shout: Come, Lord Jesus!"[7].

Discussion Guide

1. The law-freedom struggle is so evident in the New Testament. Where did the biblical writers come out on this important issue? Is it still a struggle for you?
2. The prayer of Jesus in John 17 reflects key outcomes he expected of our praying the Lord's Prayer sincerely. Exactly what outcomes does Jesus intend?

6. Snyder, "Holiness and the Five Calls of God," 151.
7. Land, *Pentecostal Spirituality*, 219.

3. What about John Wesley's house analogy? Do you understand his picture of a disciple crossing the porch, going through the door, and finally entering the house of real religion? Do you know any Christians who have done nothing but hang out on the porch? Where are you?
4. The "Holiness Manifesto" says that today's church urgently needs to renew the Christian holiness emphasis. Do you agree? How might that renewal come about?
5. Are you ready to assume the "Yes" stance in your life of faith? Put in your own words what that could mean if you actually did.
6. There is a key paragraph in this chapter that begins, "Christianity should be..." What should Christianity be?

Appendix A
The Holiness Manifesto

Background to the Manifesto

The "Holiness Manifesto" is a 2006 document written jointly by fifteen church leaders and scholars, including myself. We represented various Wesleyan, Holiness, and Pentecostal traditions of Christianity. The manifesto is intended to summarize the heart of Christian holiness beliefs, values, and practices, particularly as they appear relevant to the churches of the twenty-first century. It draws directly on biblical revelation and reflects my own deepest belief and desire.

Holiness is not a new topic; it is as old as the Bible and at the heart of what my own church tradition, the Church of God movement (Anderson), has been all about. Even so, holiness is not always a theme to which Christians are drawn for various reasons. A lull in its perceived relevance was the occasion for writing and issuing widely the manifesto.

The text of the manifesto reads as follows, with a broader history of the process that brought it into being available in an essay by Don Thorsen that I published in the fall 2007 issue of the *Wesleyan Theological Journal*. It also appears, along with a series of interpretative commentaries, in the 2008 book *The Holiness Manifesto* edited by Kevin W. Mannoia and Don Thorsen and published by the William B. Eerdmans Publishing Company, Grand Rapids, Michigan. I was privileged to author the first chapter in this book, titled "The Context: Past and Present." Now, give your attention to the manifesto itself.

The Holiness Manifesto:
The Crisis We Face

There has never been a time in greater need of a compelling articulation of the message of holiness. Pastors and church leaders at every level of the church have come to new heights of frustration in seeking ways to revitalize their congregations and denominations. What we are doing is not working. Membership in churches of all traditions has flat-lined. In many cases, churches are declining. We are not even keeping pace with the biological growth rate in North America. The power and health of churches has also been drained by the incessant search for a better method, a more effective fad, a newer and bigger program to yield growth. In the process of trying to lead growing, vibrant churches, our people have become largely ineffective and fallen prey to a generic Christianity that results in congregations that are indistinguishable from the culture around them. Churches need a clear, compelling message that will replace the "holy grail" of methods as the focus of our mission.

Many church leaders have become hostages to the success mentality of numeric and programmatic influence. They have become so concerned about "how" they do church that they have neglected the weightier matter of "what" the church declares. We have inundated the "market" with methodological efforts to grow the church. In the process, many of our leaders have lost the ability to lead. They cannot lead because they have no compelling message to give, no compelling vision of God, no transformational understanding of God's otherness. They know it and long to find the centering power of a message that makes a difference. Now more than ever, they long to soak up a deep understanding of God's call to holiness—transformed living. They want a mission. They want a message!

People all around are looking for a future without possessing a spiritual memory. They beg for a generous and integrative word from Christians that makes sense and makes a difference. If God is going to be relevant to people, we have a responsibility to make it clear to them. We have to shed our obsession with cumbersome language, awkward expectations, and intransigent patterns. What is the core, the center, the essence of God's call? That is our message, and that is our mission!

People in churches are tired of our petty lines of demarcation that artificially create compartments, denominations, and divisions. They are tired of building institutions. They long for a clear, articulate message that transcends institutionalism and in-fighting among followers of Jesus Christ. They are embarrassed by the corporate mentality of churches that defend parts of the gospel as if it were their own. They want to know the unifying power of God that transforms. They want to see the awesomeness of God's holiness that compels us to oneness in which there is a testimony of power. They accept the fact that not all of us will look alike; there will be diversity. But they want to know that churches and leaders believe that we are one—bound by the holy character of God who gives us all life and love. They want a message that is unifying. The only message that can do that comes from the nature of God, who is unity in diversity.

Therefore, in this critical time, we set forth for the church's well being a fresh focus on holiness. In our view, this focus is the heart of Scripture concerning Christian existence for all times—and clearly for our time.

The Message We Have

God is holy and calls us to be a holy people. God, who is holy, has abundant and steadfast love for us. God's holy love is revealed to us in the life and teachings, death and resurrection of Jesus Christ, our Savior and Lord. God continues to work, giving life, hope, and salvation through the indwelling of the Holy Spirit, drawing us into God's own holy, loving life. God transforms us, delivering us from sin, idolatry, bondage, and self-centeredness to love and serve God, others, and to be stewards of creation. Thus, we are renewed in the image of God as revealed in Jesus Christ.

Apart from God, no one is holy. Holy people are set apart for God's purpose in the world. Empowered by the Holy Spirit, holy people live and love like Jesus Christ. Holiness is both gift and response, renewing and transforming, personal and communal, ethical and missional. The holy people of God follow Jesus Christ in engaging all the cultures of the world and drawing all peoples to God. Holy people are not legalistic or judgmental. They do not pursue an exclusive, private state of being better than others. Holiness is not flawlessness, but the fulfillment of God's intention for us. The pursuit of holiness can never cease because love can never be exhausted.

God wants us to be, think, speak, and act in the world in a Christ-like manner. We invite all to embrace God's call to:

- be filled with all the fullness of God in Jesus Christ—Holy Spirit-endowed co-workers for the reign of God;
- live lives that are devout, pure, and reconciled, thereby being Jesus Christ's agents of transformation in the world;
- live as a faithful covenant people, building accountable community, growing up into Jesus Christ, embodying the spirit of God's law in holy love;
- exercise for the common good an effective array of ministries and callings, according to the diversity of the gifts of the Holy Spirit;
- practice compassionate ministries, solidarity with the poor, advocacy for equality, justice, reconciliation, and peace; and
- care for the earth, God's gift in trust to us, working in faith, hope, and confidence for the healing and care of all creation.

By the grace of God, let us covenant together to be a holy people.

The Action We Take

May this call impel us to rise to this biblical vision of Christian mission:

- Preach the transforming message of holiness;
- Teach the principles of Christ-like love and forgiveness;
- Embody lives that reflect Jesus Christ;
- Lead in engaging with the cultures of the world; and
- Partner with others to multiply its effect for the reconciliation of all things.

For this we live and labor to the glory of God.

Appendix B

Three Insights from the Lord's Prayer

In 2010, Dr. Thomas E. Phillips published his book *God Heard That!* He puts at the head of the list of prayers heard by God the Lord's Prayer, the one God will always hear with appreciation when it is offered thoughtfully and honestly. Having for many years prayed this prayer taught by Jesus, and usually three times daily, Phillips concludes his comments on this classic prayer with a few things that he has learned. They are worth noting by all of us.

> First, *if I want to understand what this world should be like, I have to look beyond it*. There is a place—heaven—where God dwells and where the Father's will is done. If the places of my life are ever to look like that place, that miracle will come only through prayer.
>
> Second, *I am privileged*. I've never been really hungry, at least not to the point of true bodily distress. I've never seen a day without bread, but other people have. If you're privileged like me and you pray "give us our daily bread" three times each day, wait and see what happens. I bet you'll become uncomfortably aware of two things, that you already have all the bread that you really need and that Christ calls us to help those who do not.
>
> Third, *the more that I plead for forgiveness, the easier it is to forgive*. When someone—even a guy like me—pleads for forgiveness three times a day, something wonderful happens. A genuine, kind, and loving spirit of forgiveness wells up naturally in the heart of the truly forgiven. It's hard to

remain unforgiving when you thrice daily pray, "forgive us our trespasses."

Finally, *the first step in overcoming temptation is avoiding temptation*. There are places I cannot comfortably go and things that I cannot really do while I am praying "lead us not into temptation." It's easier to avoid such places and activities when I sincerely pray this prayer. These words lead me away from temptation.

Bibliography

Barclay, William. *The Lord's Prayer*, Insight. Edinburgh, Scotland: St. Andrew Press, 2008.

Callen, Barry L. "The Context: Past and Present." In *The Holiness Manifesto*, edited by Kevin Mannoia and Don Thorsen, 8–17. Grand Rapids, MI: Wm. B. Eerdmans, 2008.

Crossan, John Dominic. *The Greatest Prayer*. New York: HarperOne, 2010.

Day, Gardiner M. *The Lord's Prayer: An Interpretation*. Greenwich, CT: Seabury Press, 1954.

Gafney, Leo. *A Guide to the "Our Father" Today*. New York: Paulist Press, 2006.

Hart,. Mark. *The "R" Father: 14 Ways to Respond to the Lord's Prayer*. Frederick, MD: Word Among Us Press, 2010.

Jones, E. Stanley. *A Song of Ascents*. Nashville, TN: Abingdon Press, 1968.

Jones, Kenneth E. *Commitment to Holiness*. Anderson, IN: Warner Press, 1985.

Kendall, R. T. *The Lord's Prayer*. Grand Rapids, MI: Chosen, 2010.

Killinger, John. *The God Named Hallowed*. Nashville, TN: Abingdon Press, 1983.

Land, Steven J. *Pentecostal Spirituality*. Sheffield, England: Sheffield Academic Press, 1993.

Laymon, Charles M. *The Lord's Prayer in Its Biblical Setting*. Nashville, TN: Abingdon Press, 1968.

Liverett, David. *Light from the Barn*. Anderson, IN: Chinaberry House, 2006.

Manning, Brennan. *The Signature of Jesus*. Rev. ed. Sisters, OR: Multnomah, 1996.

Mannoia, Kevin W., and Don Thorsen, eds. *The Holiness Manifesto*. Grand Rapids, MI: William B. Eerdmans, 2008.

Merton, Thomas. *No Man Is an Island*. Boston: Shambhala, 2005.

Migliore, Daniel L., ed., *The Lord's Prayer*. Grand Rapids, MI: Eerdmans, 1993.

Moltmann, Jürgen. *Jesus Christ for Today's World*. Minneapolis, MN: Fortress Press, 1994.

Murray, Andrew. *With Christ in the School of Prayer*. Radford, VA: Wilder Publications Ltd.

Newberry, Gene W. *A Boy from Lewis County*. Privately published, 2000.

Packer, J. I. *Praying the Lord's Prayer*. Wheaton, IL: Crossway Books, 2007.

Phillips, Thomas E. *God Heard That!* Privately published, 2010.

Pinnock, Clark H. *Flame of Love: A Theology of the Holy Spirit*. Downer's Grove, IL: InterVarsity Press, 1996.

Ryken, Philip Graham. *The Prayer of Our Lord*. Wheaton, IL: Crossway Books, 2002.

Schweitzer, Albert. *The Quest of the Historical Jesus*. Rev. ed. Minneapolis, MN: Fortress Press, 2001.

Seamands, Stephen A. *Holiness of Heart and Life*. Nashville, TN: Abingdon Press, 1990.

Snyder, Howard A. "Holiness and the Five Calls of God: Holiness in Postmodernity." In *The Holiness Manifesto*, edited by Kevin Mannoia and Don Thorsen, 129–151. Grand Rapids, MI: Wm. B. Eerdmans, 2008.

Sproul, R. C. *The Prayer of the Lord*. Orlando, FL: Reformation Trust, 2009.

Timms, David. *Living the Lord's Prayer*. Minneapolis, MN: Bethany House, 2008.

———. *Sacred Waiting*. Minneapolis, MN: Bethany House, 2009.

Trueblood, D. Elton. *The Lord's Prayers*. New York: Harper & Row, 1965.

Wesleyan Holiness Study Project. "The Holiness Manifesto." In *The Holiness Manifesto*, edited by Kevin W. Mannoia and Don Thorsen. Grand Rapids, MI: William B. Eerdmans Company, 2008.

Wiersbe, Warren W. *On Earth as It Is in Heaven*. Grand Rapids, MI: Baker Books, 2010.

Willimon, William, and Stanley Hauerwas. *Lord, Teach Us*. Nashville, TN: Abingdon Press, 1996.

Wilkinson, Bruce. *The Prayer of Jabez*. Sisters, OR: Multnomah Publishers, 2000.

Wright, N. T. *The Lord and His Prayer*. Grand Rapids, MI: Eerdmans Publishing, 1996.

Zodhiates, Spiros. *The Lord's Prayer*. Chattanooga, TN: AMG Publisher, 1982, 1983.